I0162116

Freedom Words International Publishers
Miami & Johannesburg

FWIP

Mailing Address:
PMB 565250
Miami, FL 33256-7215

To those who served and to those who dissented

Author royalties from the sale of this book will
be donated to
The Vietnam Veterans Memorial Fund

Step Forward The Hero

Contents

Preface

This story rightly begins on a personal note for it is the fulfillment of a promise made to the father of Milton L. Olive, III, back in the late 1970s. I was in attendance at the ceremony in Chicago at which a park was being named in honor of young Milton Olive. At the end of that event, I had the great pleasure to speak with the senior Olive and share with him my thoughts about his son whose heroism I knew of when it was first announced in our hometown of Chicago in 1965 that he would be posthumously awarded the Medal of Honor. The young Milton and I were roughly the same age when he dropped out of high school and went off to Vietnam and I stayed in high school and

then went off to college. In speaking with the
father I mentioned to him that I had recently
completed my doctorate in history and was on my
way to a new teaching position. He wished me
well and then challenged me to "Please someday
do a book about my son. Future generations of
young people need to know about him." With the
following pages I proudly honor that longstanding commitment.

The reader is reminded that the period 2013-
2015 marks the 40th anniversary of the ending of
the Vietnam War (Paris Peace Accords signed in
1973 to the final halting of hostilities in 1975).
The year 2015 also marks the 50th anniversary and
commemoration of young Milton Olive's
heroism and sacrifice.

Chapter 1:

At Home in Chicago and

Mississippi

It was the fourth time this semester that a fight broke out in the Milton L Olive Middle School. The Long Island New York school seemed to be plagued with violence. This particular brawl involved at least sixteen students and resembled an old Western barroom brawl. The little tykes, most of them twelve or thirteen years of age, were going at it throwing blows, books, back packs, and scratching, punching, and kicking. If that was not bad enough, two of the students started brandishing knifes. If it was not for the swift intervention of Mr. Jamison, someone could have been seriously injured or even killed.

Other teachers started running out of their classrooms to the scene of the brawl but Jamison had it under control. When he yelled to students to "stop it now!" they obeyed instantly. He only had to say it one time. His voice carried that clearly and with that much authority. Even though he had been teaching at the school for only two years, he had already gained a reputation as a no-nonsense disciplinarian. He commanded respect in and out of the classroom. That he stood six feet four inches and weighed as much as a small truck might have also had something to do with it. But brawn was not the only thing he possessed. He loved students and the discipline of history.

With the sixteen brawlers now under control and attentive, Mr. Jamison directed them to come into his classroom although the school day was near officially over with only fifteen minutes to go before 2:30 p.m. and the ending bell. Jamison was always among the last teachers to leave the building and if he had not been there who knows what the outcome of the rumble might have been.

He told the students to take a seat and that he wanted to speak to them. There were moans and groans but Jamison pretended he did not hear any of it. His first attention went with the two students who brandished knives. Rather than report them or call the police or tell the principal, Jamison simply gave them the alternative of either turning the knives over to him or that he would report them to law enforcement. The two students in question relinquished their blades, with Jamison giving them stares that told them in no uncertain terms that their behavior was far beyond the boundaries of acceptability. He could have had them expelled from school but, as usual for him, he saw this too as a teaching opportunity and especially one to pass on his love of history to his captive audience.

The sixteen youngsters were a good statistical representation of the makeup of the Olive Middle School which was predominately African American.   Nine of sixteen were African American; four were white, and three Hispanic. There were not only boys but girls. Even the girls were fierce brawlers at the school.

Mr. Jamison had a simple question that he asked the sixteen and told them that once they answered it for him he would let them go home. His question was: What were they fighting about? Receiving no answer except some shrugs of the shoulders and some students looking like they may have had an answer but not willing to share it, he went on to his second question and he prefaced it by saying that he wanted to talk to them not just as a teacher but as a black man, a person of color with unique sensitivities and one dedicated to the advancement of his students no matter what their race, creed, color or economic disadvantages.

Having laid that framework, he then said to them: "Here you are at the Milton L Olive Middle School and you are wasting the educational opportunity of a lifetime. How many of you even know who Milton L Olive was? Can anyone answer that for me?"

There was dead silence. Then finally one student raised her hand. Jamison knew it was Shanekwa since she was one of his history students, and he knew she knew the answer to the question since he always started the new semester by telling his students about the school's namesake.

"Shanekwa, since you are in my class and know who Olive was, I am not calling on you."

"Why were you fighting?" Jamison asked.

Shanekwa answered that she was not fighting but was trying to rescue her girl friend from the crowd. Jamison, knowing that she was a good student, believed her and told her that she could leave if she wanted to without having to hear his lecture again about Milton Olive.

"That's okay, Mister J., I wouldn't mind hearing it again. It's a great story," Shanekwa answered, and set back down.

The others, Jamison gave a choice. If they did not want to stay and hear about Milton Olive, he would report them all to the principal, and the two who brandished knifes, he was going to immediately report to the police. "You are free to leave if you want to," Jamison offered.

Not surprisingly, there were no takers. "Okay, then, let me tell you about Milton L. Olive, the person for whom our school is named. You should know about him not just because our school is named after him. You should know about him because he gave his life for his friends and for our country! He was not that much older than you when he died. He was a teenager, like several of you are and the rest of you will be too in a few years."

The students were completely silent and attentive as Jamison began telling them the story of Milton L. Olive.

Milton Lee Olive, III, was born November 7, 1946, in Lexington, Mississippi, at the hands of a midwife. His mother, Clara Lee, died giving him birth. Milton was a breach birth and what we would call today a prenatal or premature baby. Certainly it seemed that way in terms of his size.

He was tiny and barely over four pounds when he was born. So, to say the least, Milton's beginning was a tenuous one; he was lucky to be alive, and frail as could be.

Milton's father, Milton B. Olive, Jr., was devastated by the loss of his wife. In her honor he gave his new son as a middle name, the name Lee, which had been his wife's maiden name. He also gave Milton his name of Milton Olive, designating him III. Those first months of life for the baby were touch and go. He was a sickly child from the beginning, and health concerns dominated his early years. The family would not stop thinking constantly about his health issues until he was almost a teenager.

It was no easy matter for his widowed father to raise a son on his own. The extended family was crucial in young Milton's development and early life. His grandmother, Eva L. Olive, and grandfather, Milton B. Olive, Sr., were surrogate parents in the raising of their grandson especially during those first years.

After Milton Olive, Jr. moved with his young son to Chicago, and took of residence at 6012 South Loomis, the extended family there would play a critical role. Olive junior's brother also lived in Chicago, and he and his wife often took care of the youngster for days at a time when the father needed a hand owing to his work schedule at the General Motors Electro-Motive Division in La Grange and later with the Chicago Department of Human Services.

There was also the help of other relatives and family friends in the neighborhood, which included Jacob Augustus Spencer and Zelphia Wareagle Spencer, who young Milton called "Big Mama." There were George and Ruth Spencer, and cousins Charles, Barbara, and Chinta.

Antoinette Mainor, a graduate of Spelman College and public school teacher in the Windy City, became young Milton's loving stepmother when his father remarried in 1952.

Crucial were the youngster's grandparents back in Lexington. During his childhood and teenage years, young Milton went back and forth between Lexington and Chicago. Several times he stayed with the grandparents for the better part of an entire year. He attended school in both Lexington and Chicago, with the vast majority of his schooling and playing hours taking place in the Windy City.

Young Milton was in many respects a frustrated youngster in that he never competed in sports and no one was likely to choose him even for a game of basketball in the playground. It was tough for him.

"Do you know how it feels not to be selected when the guys you know are choosing teams?" Mr. Jamison asked the students. "Milton was virtually never selected. He was left out of the game of basketball which, in black Chicago, was 'the' game."

"Yes, you bet," several of the students replied in almost unison. They knew how bad it must have hurt young Milton not to have been chosen when his friends were selecting teams. At least Milton never experienced bullying from his classmates.

In his south side neighborhood of Englewood, basketball was supreme just as it was throughout the Windy City's black communities. In high school, he wanted very much to try out for the football team and the basketball squad. Even at the parochial school he attended, Mount Travancore, he was much too small for football and basketball. He could have tried out for the wrestling squad since that was based on weight but he did not possess the competitive attitude and toughness for wrestling. Milton was the kind of teen more likely to be on the chess team than on the football or basketball squad. Chess, however, was not that popular in either the parochial school or the public schools he also attended in later years.

He would carry that kind of negative in his mind throughout his school years. His father never focused on that issue. He was much more concerned with just getting his son a good education. When in Mississippi, young Milton attended a school run by the Pentecostal church in Lexington, which, by all indications, he did not like very much. Neither was he that fond of the Nicholas Copernicus Parochial School that he later attended in Chicago.

At the same time, his father doted on young Milton. He made sure that his son had bicycles and toy train sets and BB guns, and that he was always immaculately dressed. Relatives noted that even as a youngster Milton and his father wore matching suits. There was love and a father who wanted the very best for his young son.

Young Milton's greatest passion growing up was photography. It began when his father gave him a new Kodak camera for his tenth birthday. He took pictures of everything from family members to birds in flight, buildings, and people on the streets. Photography caught the imagination of the youngster. He loved the capturing of life in a moment of stillness that preserved the scene forever. He was good at experimenting with taking shots at various angles and with different apertures. Milton's daytime photos were playful and exhilarating portraits.

His evening shots he thought of as mysterious and quiet with a beauty as great as those he took in daylight.   Milton's father would give his son several more cameras over the years. Photography was something that the youngster stuck with and loved as an expression of who he was. When he was twelve, Milton's father had a business card made up as a gift to his son. Milton would keep that card with him. He cherished the card not only as a gift from his father but as a testament to a budding visual artist. The card read: "Milton L. Olive, III, The Youngest Professional Photographer in Chicago."

Milton came of age in a very interesting time in our nation's history; a time that encompassed the civil rights movement. On one of his stays in Mississippi, he became very interested in the struggle and other aspects of the black movement for equality in America.   He thought that in

Mississippi he would work to help solve the problem.

His grandparents lived in Dixie but they had a decent life, their own home and a bit of property. They were not poor by the standards of the day. They would have been easily classified as lower middle to middle class. They would have also been classified as the kind of blacks who did not want to stir up any trouble.

It was a contradiction that Milton was starting to feel every time he went to the South. He knew how things were in Chicago and that blacks there had problems. They also had a very different attitude from those in Mississippi. Black Chicagoans did not step off the sidewalk when a white person passed or give up their seat on the bus, nor drink from colored only water fountains. In short, there were problems in the Windy City but certainly the difference between blacks living there and blacks living in Mississippi were worlds apart.

An incident, as he was starting to approach his teen years, that stood out in his young mind was when he and some friends there in Lexington went into a local store to buy candy, ice cream and soda pop. The two friends, paying before him, both addressed the young white male clerk, who was only maybe a few years older than them, as sir. When it was Milton's turn to pay and the individual gave him his change back, he took it and started to walk out the store. The young white behind the counter said to him, "What do you say?" Milton replied, "What do you mean, what do I say?" The young white boy told him that he had not said "Thank you sir." Milton thought this was very strange since this young boy was about the same age as he and it was Milton who was buying something and thus the one entitled to the thanks if any.

That only made sense to young Milton and he turned and started to walk out of the store. The young white behind the counter spoke in an even louder voice to the whole group. He said to Milton's friends, "You should tell him how we do things down here. I can tell he's not from around these parts and he better learn quickly." Milton's two friends began profusely addressing the white boy with "Thank you sir, we will. Thank you sir. We will be sure, yes."

They exited the store. Outside, Milton's friends told him that he needed to learn how things worked in Mississippi and stop with his Chicago ways. "You got to tell everybody, every white person, 'yes sir and no sir; yes ma'am and no ma'am." Milton told them that he did that with grown people but not with children. He also asked, "Why would I say that to someone my own age? He's no older than we are."

His friends retorted, "That's the way of doing things here in Mississippi. You can get in a lot of trouble if you don't follow the rules."

They were of course correct about the fact that if a black person failed to show appropriate demeanor and acquiescence to any white person he or she could be in serious jeopardy.

When Milton got back to his grandparents' place he told them the story thinking that they would immediately be on his side. Not only were they not on his side, they were horrified at what he told them and that he had failed to pay sufficient homage to the young white clerk. They knew only too well what could be the consequences in Mississippi if any white person felt that they had been insulted by a Negro.

The grandparents immediately started in on Milton with a lecture about what had happened to a black youngster who came down from Chicago just a few years ago and who was not much older than him.   That youngster failed to show appropriate humility and homage to a white woman clerk in a store. Later that evening, two white men came to the youngster's home, where he was visiting his uncle in Money, Mississippi, and took him from the house at gunpoint. His body was found days later. He had been beaten, mutilated, and shot through the head, and his body dumped into the river. That young black male was named Emmett Till.

Milton knew of the Till story. He was 9 years old when it happened and he heard his father and others talk about it in Chicago. He remembered the outpouring of indignation all around the Windy City black community and the funeral for young Till held on Chicago's south side. He heard about the long lines of mourners who came to the chapel to pay their respects. He remembered, only too well, the vivid picture of the mutilated Till that appeared on the cover of *Jet Magazine*, which he looked at over and over again. It was too horrible to believe. The young boy's face was unrecognizable, swollen, beaten in, and crushed. Yet Till's mother insisted that he receive an open casket funeral. She did so because, as she said, "I want the world to see what they did to my boy."

Racism was real in Milton's world, especially in the South of that era. It could turn violent at any moment on the slightest whim or innuendo. His grandparents knew this and debated long and hard whether they should immediately return him to Chicago. At that particular time, they decided not to with assurances from him that he would show appropriate approbation whenever going into a store or coming in contact with whites in Lexington.   Milton, although reluctantly, kept that promise at first and tried to adapt as much as he could to the ways of his southern kinfolk with the proper 'yes sir' or 'yes ma'am' to any white person no matter what their age. He was getting a lesson on behavior in the deep South for a black person.

But each time Milton went home to Chicago whether it was for a month or more or less, he would be infused with a new vigor and manliness that he brought back to Mississippi. It had the potential of putting him in danger. He was doing his best when he came back to the South to act accordingly but he was finding that more and more difficult as the 1960s emerged and he matured with the times. It was while in Lexington at the age of fifteen that he became fascinated with the sequence of events that had the potential of making a man out of him, or perhaps getting him killed.

It was the beginning of the 1960s and the fight for civil rights reached a fever pitch in the South. Dr. Martin Luther King, Jr. had become a household name. There were massive civil rights marches and protests taking place such as in Birmingham, Alabama, in 1963. That same year and in the same city, four little black girls, Adie Mae Collins, Denise McNair, Carole Robertson, and Cynthia Wesley, were killed when a racist bombed the Sixteenth Street Baptist Church. Medgar Evers, the NAACP leader in Mississippi, was shot in the back and killed in front of his house. All of this meant that in places like Mississippi, tensions were high and the lines drawn in the sand by white racists who were determined to protect the status quo and to keep the color line in place.

Freedom Summer of 1964 marked Milton's last days in Lexington. While back with his grandparents, he clandestinely became actively involved in the Freedom Vote Campaign to register black voters. He attended one of the Freedom Schools that summer and participated in the efforts of CORE (Congress of Racial Equality) and S NCC (Student Nonviolent Coordinating Committee) in their voter registration drives; all of this, despite being too young to vote himself. Nevertheless he understood the importance of the ballot and why it was so crucial for black people to stand up and demand their fair share in America. The major push to get blacks registered to vote in the South struck a powerful cord with young Milton. He got involved, attended meetings, and more than once went out into the local community urging black folk to register and to vote. He may not have been an intellectual student of the civil rights protests, nonviolent direct action, and the need for social change, yet he knew that what these groups stood for was right and that it was time for change.

When three CORE workers, James Chaney, Andrew Goodman, and Michael Schwerner, were killed in Mississippi later that year, Milton's grandparents decided that he had to return to Chicago. They wrote to his father and told him that they were "scared for Milton and for themselves." His father ordered him back to Chicago and he complied.

It would be nice to say that Milton's father understood the importance of the civil rights movement and was somehow involved and connected himself. He was not. Like his kinfolk in Lexington, despite him living in Chicago, Milton's father was no activist. Moreover, he wanted his son to stay clear of those things that had the potential of getting him killed, and he felt that the civil rights movement and involvement in it, especially in Mississippi, could do just that. Milton's father had a point; no question about it. But this was a time of change and challenge and his son Milton, even at his young age, felt an affinity toward the movement to make America live up to its lofty stated principles of freedom, equality, and justice for all. That belief, however, got young Milton sent back to Chicago and the confrontation with his father that would be a turning point in his life.

Milton's father set down with him on more than one occasion and laid down the law: that what he was doing in Mississippi was too dangerous for him to be involved in and that he did not want to see him hurt. Milton's father took the position that to toe the line, work hard, keep your nose clean, get an education, and you can make it in this world.

His son disagreed, respectfully. Milton took the position that the fight belonged to everyone and that it was up to each and every black person and white person who believed in freedom and equality to take a stand against what was going on in the South. He told his father that he thought it was their turn to stand up for what was right.

"Son, I love you, and I don't want to see you dead," said Milton's father. "This nation of ours has its problems and nowhere is that more true than in the Jim Crow South. Don't forget young man, I was born down there. I lived my youth and my early adult years in Mississippi. You heard me tell the story before, and the reason I came up here to Chicago was to get away from the hell of Mississippi. My family had it better than a lot of other Negroes down there. We owned our house and a little piece of land and were getting by. We were not wealthy people of course but I would say we were close to a kind of middle class, working class folks. We were doing all right but you had to mind your P's and Q's in good old Mississippi. Everybody knew that if you got too far out of line you had the likelihood of being hung. That is not the thing I wanted for my children. That's the major reason that I came north, that I came to Chicago. Your mother and I used to talk about this all the time. I know the problems, but the opportunity for learning here is far greater than down South. We want you to be able to go to a really good school. That's the reason we send you to a parochial school. That costs money as you know. We're not rich people but I will put forth whatever is necessary for my son, you, to have a good life. I'm disappointed that you don't love education and strive to be the very best in your class. I am hurt that even right now you're telling me that you don't like school."

"Well, dad, I am not sure about school," Milton replied. "The problem is that so much is going on right now that calls for us taking a stand and trying to make a difference. When I'm in school down in Lexington you can see it, you can feel it even though it is not seen in the schoolhouse, it is off campus. We talked about these things. The movement is alive even in Mississippi. I really think you have to take a stand and fight. A lot of the kids doing this are my age and even younger than me and are right there on the front lines. I want to fight for what I believe in. I appreciate all that you and Mom have done for me. Mom gave me life and gave up her life to give me life. I will never forget that. I know that you struggle each day to make my life better and I appreciate it. I want to make all of our lives better and I think I can do that by being involved, by getting out there, by trying to make a difference."

"Son, I appreciate all that you say. The problem is, and I repeat, the white folks in Mississippi will kill you. You won't do anybody any good if you are dead." Milton's father made a powerful point, but his son likewise was making some valid observations and some strong arguments for people to stand up and fight for what they believed and, if necessary, to put their lives on the line.

Young Milton knew about Medgar Evers and the many other civil rights leaders who were killed, jailed, and the countless demonstrators who were abused and who faced up against dogs, high pressure water hoses, police billy clubs, and angry whites who long after the marches stopped were still going around intimidating black folk, burning down their houses and planting bombs to blow them up. He felt that now was the time, if there ever was a time, to stand up and fight back.

One thing young Milton was not: he was not a coward. Anyone who knew him knew that the young man had guts. He may have been quiet for the most part and someone who seemed to blend into the background rather than a force out front, but there was fire in his belly. He was a determined individual when it came to standing up for principles. It is not to suggest that his father was not also a principled individual. It is just that his father had the burden of fatherhood and, in a sense, motherhood as well despite his supportive second wife; and he took it to mean that his first priority was to keep his son safe.

The senior Milton was a churchgoer, not an overly devout Christian person, but one who did believe in God and the hereafter. Young Milton on occasion accompanied his father to church or with one of the other relatives there in Chicago, and certainly with the relatives when in Lexington. Always after church, whether it was in Lexington or Chicago, there would be good food and a feeling of joyousness around the house. It was on one of those occasions back home in Chicago that he and his father had their first opportunity to sit down and actually talk about God and the hereafter.

Young Milton initiated the discussion. Minister Delong had given a rousing sermon that afternoon, in the tradition of the black Baptist church, full of call-and-response: "Can I get a witness?" "Tell the truth now," "Well," and plenty of "Amens." Now, sitting there in their small living room, father and son alone, both still dressed in their suits and ties, exchanged ideas about the meaning of God, prayer, and the church.

Was there a God?   If so, why did God not intervene in the struggle for human rights?   Why didn't God save those black men from being lynched? Why didn't God protect those four little girls from the bomber?   Why didn't God protect those black women from being assaulted?   The father and his son were exchanging ideas rapidly and, in a sense, enjoying the lively exchange. What was clear to any outside listener would have been the inescapable fact that both were religious and that the son may have actually been more religious than his father.

"God is real for me," the young Milton assured his father.

"I know it son," senior replied.

What both of them were wrestling with was the question of why was there not divine intervention in the plight of black people? They both could cite the standard answer that most religious people typically give: "God works in mysterious ways." But neither father nor son were accepting of that at the moment. They both raised questions about the "why."

"Dad, I'm telling you, the only way I can figure it is that there must be some larger plan that none of us are privy to."

"Son, I think you have a point. I've often said that. When your Mother died, the only way I could make sense out of her death was to think that God must have a master plan and we were just not privileged to know the plan. Because I tell you I have a difficult time understanding how there could be a God and to take your mother away from me and, more importantly, to take her away from her newborn child."

The two sat quietly, not really looking at one another, staring off into the gaze of contemplation and wonderment. The words that each said had triggered deep emotions and called for profound reflection.   They both knew that they had no answer to the secret of the universe.   They both knew that they were hungry for better understanding, but that it might only come through their faith in themselves and to powers beyond themselves.

Milton may have said it best, when he told his father: "My mother is with me.   I have always felt that she never really left me.   I've always felt that someone was looking over my shoulder saying do this, do that, don't do this, don't do that.   It may have just been me talking to myself, but I believe it was her, her spirit speaking within me.   No, she never left me.   She never left us.   She may have departed this earth in her physical form, but a spirit lives on forever and certainly as long as you and I and everyone who knew her live."

Senior rose from his chair and took two long steps around the table and grabbed his son by the hand and started pulling him up. The young Milton rose and the two embraced not like two long-lost friends who had not seen each other after many years, but a slow embrace with a strong hug from each that nearly pushed the breath out of both. They were on the same wavelength. The death of Clara Lee had not diminished their faith. It strengthened the bond between the father and his son, despite their differences on participating in the civil rights movement.

When back home in Chicago, young Milton picked up occasional afterschool jobs. They were minimum wage but it was work. When he was down in Lexington, his work was around the family farm and that consisted of everything from helping to milk cows to bailing hay, feeding the hogs, cleaning the barn, feeding the chickens, and fetching wood. Despite that great exercise, he still seemed to get no taller than his 5'6" and no bigger than his 125 or so pounds. But his spirit seemed to grow in stature and confidence. Relegated to Chicago, after his involvement with the civil rights struggle in Mississippi, the question was what was he going to do permanently with his life?

What he kept with him from the Mississippi trips was the nickname his grandma Eva Olive dubbed him. It started when he was around twelve, calling him Skipper. Speculation was that she dubbed him that because he loved to skip rocks in the nearby pond. Others say she nicknamed him that because he played hooky from school so often, skipping classes because he found them unfulfilling. Perhaps Grandma Olive called him Skipper because he was never in one place permanently, skipping from Chicago to Lexington and from Lexington back to Chicago. Whatever the true origins of his nickname, it stuck. Family and friends alike called him Skipper, except for his father, who preferred addressing his son by his given name of Milton.

In school, Milton was at best an average student. He seemed to like school less in Lexington than in Chicago but often skipped out on both. The nature of the curriculum of the Pentecostal school in Mississippi certainly differed from that up North. It was mainly about a farmer's way of life and basic reading and writing and arithmetic. He got much more of a traditional liberal arts education in Chicago. But neither one completely satisfied him. It was as if his mind was preoccupied elsewhere. He wanted more, but he was not devoted to the notion of education as the means to achieve his future goals. This no doubt contributed to why Milton did not excel in class. The fire in the belly was not there for him when it came to formal education. If he had been attending a school devoted to photography, perhaps it would have been a different story.

"I bet that some of you feel that way about classes you are taking?" Jamison interrupted his story-telling to make a relevant point. "Is that correct or not?"

"Amend again!" one of the students shouted out, which brought considerable laughter.

"The key," Jamison continued, "is to embrace everything that your teachers are trying to give you. Take advantage of the opportunity. As you get older, you will be able to focus more on what it is that you like, and what you want to be. You have to have the basics first. Please don't forget that. No matter how boring or difficult you find a particular class or subject, keep with it. Education is the key."

"Well, why didn't Milton understand that?" Yousef asked. Then he answered his own question: "I think he didn't understand the value of education because he didn't like the education they were giving him. Pentecostal or Catholic or Baptist, the white man's religion and his schools won't make you smart."

"What do you think of what Yousef just said?" Jamison asked of the group. There was silence and Jamison decided not to push the issue. He would let them think about it and perhaps come back to that question later. For now, he continued on with the story of Milton Olive.

Young Milton had his passions: his belief in God, his belief in his father, his belief in his grandparents and other relatives, and his desire to be something more than the short, frail kid who no one picked to be on their playground basketball team.

Many called the age of 16 as being sweet 16. That was never the case for Skipper. Sixteen would prove to be his most difficult year because it is later after his 16th birthday that the discussions between he and his father escalated to almost a daily routine of questioning what he wanted to be and what he wanted to do with his life. Senior believed that his son was starting to go adrift. He envisioned great things for Milton and that was one of the reasons he doted on him with gifts all through his childhood and paid the heavy price of putting him into private school. It appeared that Milton was going to be just average and his father, to say the least, was terribly disappointed. In many of their frank discussions, senior would ask: "What are you going to do with your life? I want great things for you. How do we make that happen? What do you want to be when you are a man?"

In a very real sense, junior had not answered those questions even to himself. He was still in the feeling-out-years of his life, trying to decipher the world of ideas around him, the conflicts of a society that promised equal opportunity to all yet denied it to him and his race. He was yet to find himself. He was in an era where finding yourself was quite permissible certainly if you were Caucasian. He, however, was not a young Caucasian. He was a young black male in a changing world with always fewer opportunities, but with a father and extended family that wanted the very best for him. What would he be when he grew up? His father was constantly asking him to answer that important question. It was during one of those evenings that senior started to hint at what would become a constant theme throughout that year: "Son, you have to make a decision about what you are going to do with your life!"

As he turned 17 that November, Skipper made a decision. He decided that school was not for him. He did not find intellectual, moral, ethical, or any kind of definitive answers for himself in school in Chicago and did not find it when attending school in Lexington. The answer did not come in church for him either. He read his Bible and kept one with him in his room and when he traveled and went down South. He found solace in many of the Scriptures. Eluding him was the answer to the most pressing question of "Who am I and what am I meant to do?"

It was during the winter in Chicago that his father finally gave him a man-sized ultimatum. Winter in Chicago can be very cold. The city is not known as the Windy City for no reason. Homes were made very tight to maintain the heat and brace inhabitants against the devastating chills coming off of Lake Michigan and the subzero temperatures that dropped even further as they were pushed on by the "hawk," which black Chicagoans nicknamed the wind of the Windy City. It had been pretty tough that January and one only ventured outside to either go to work or go to school or for some special reason. You simply did not go outside in the bitter cold unless necessity demanded. It was during the cold spell that Skipper made his decision that he was going to drop out of school. It was over dinner while he and his father were talking about mapping out some sort of future for him that he informed his father: "Dad, I've come to a decision. I don't want to go on any further in school."

His father was shocked by this news and urged him to reconsider noting that he was approaching his senior year and should at least finish high school. Milton responded that school was unfulfilling to him, that he was not a great student; he was bored to death, had no close friends there and felt totally unfulfilled in school in both Chicago and in Lexington.

This is one of the rare occasions when his father lost control. He did not yell. What he gave his son was an ultimatum. He told Milton that he could go to school, get a job, or go into the military.

"The choice is yours son," his father said. "Every man has to pull his weight. Now I haven't asked you to contribute to the family coffers or anything like that as long as you were going to school. But if you're not going to school, then you have to work full time and do your part and contribute to the household budget. I hope you decide to go on to school and get an education, even go on to college.

"Son you could be a doctor or lawyer or a professor, or if not get a good skill and get a really good paying job. I tell you this, you can't just sit around. You can't just be a part of what's going on down South, of being involved in that civil rights mess. So there's your choice: school, work, or the military!"

There it was, the ultimatum, the showdown, the final take it or leave it. Senior was demanding that his son grow up and be a man even though he was only 17 years of age. His father was not a tyrant and he did not demand that his son give him an immediate answer, although it may have seemed that way to Milton. The ultimatum hung over Milton's head for several months, sometimes with a certain intensity in senior's voice and other times with a gentleness that was almost a plea that his son go the education route rather than either work or the military.

One can only guess at how Skipper made his final decision. Did he conclude that he hated school so much that he was not going to be good at it? Did he not aspire to be a professional such as a physician, a lawyer, a professor, a dentist, an engineer or something? Why did he not decide that if the civil rights movement was his passion, to move down South no matter what his grandparents or father said? He could have joined CORE or SNCC. He did neither. Milton L Olive, III, was a youngster who had not found himself. He was indecisive as many young people are at that particular time in life. He did not know what he wanted to be when he grew up, and that was the problem.

There were many nights that he lay awake thinking about the future, thinking about the present and thinking about what he would do next. Having not found fulfillment in the academic world, the world of ideas, his choice would either be the workplace or the military. Most of the work for uneducated black males was as common laborers, and in that capacity size did matter. He was always small with a physique that gave no hint of the physical strength to put in a rigorous eight hour day, day in and day out. Any employer would have been able to see that, and Skipper knew it. In that regard, it was clear that he knew to some degree, his own limitations.

He concluded that he needed an environment where if accepted he could make his mark, and he would do so. He needed an environment that would not depend on physical strength alone. Required was an environment in which he could be measured by his performance when given an equal chance. Make no mistake about it, young Milton did not harbor an inferiority complex when it came to his own self-worth. He knew he would never be a great athlete. On the other hand, he could contribute and make a difference. The only question was where.

Like all of us, if we are to have a fulfilling life, we need to be able to find what it is that makes us tick, what it is that we are willing to get up for in the morning, put in long hours, and devote ourselves. These were the points of reference that drove Skipper. He wanted to know who he was. He wanted to prove himself not only to himself but to those whom he loved, namely his family and friends, and especially his father.

Milton made his decision. Of the three alternatives his father gave him: education, work, or the military, the 17 year old decided that he would join the United States Army.

"Did his father make him join the army?" a student asked.

"What is your name?"

"My name is Cynthia."

"His father gave him an ultimatum and gave him three choices, one of which was to go into the military. His father really wanted him to choose education and, following that, to choose work. Senior had no idea that his small son would choose the macho alternative of the military," Jamison answered.

"I don't think that it was his father's fault that he chose the military," Cynthia concluded.

"A great many young men in the past and now today even women go into the military in hope of building the future. When Milton went into the military in 1964, his hope was just that," Jamison responded.

"Mister Jamison don't you think he made a mistake?" Cynthia asked.

Before Jamison could reply, an answer came from another student.

"Damn right he made a mistake. He went to war for a nation that didn't even treat him like an equal." The comments came from Yousef.

"Yousef, are you a Muslim?" Jamison asked.

"No. My folks just didn't want me to have another one of those slave names like Albert, David, Sean, or Jamison."

The students started laughing.

"I was just asking because your comment was so hard-hitting and to the point," Jamison replied.

"My folks," Yousef retorted, "think for black folks to fight in the white man's wars is crazy. This brother, what was his name, Milton, Milton Olive? He should never have put on the white man's uniform; that's what my grandfather says all the time. We should not be fighting for a country that is really not ours."

"Are there others of you who agree with Yousef?" Jamison inquired.

"I most certainly do. It does not make sense to fight for a place that treats us the way this country has," Yousef blurted out despite Jamison putting the question to others.

Yousef was making a strong point and there were those students who were nodding their heads in agreement with what he said.

"I understand what you mean," Jamison responded. "But Milton saw the world differently than you or your grandfather and perhaps your parents."

"Then I think he was a fool," Yousef fired back. "This is not our country and we have no business fighting for it."

Yousef was standing his ground and Jamison was not attempting to make him change his mind as much as he wanted him to explore it more fully and get the rest of the class involved in the discussion.

It did not take long. Another student raised her hand and blurted out: "I disagree. My older brother is in Afghanistan right now, fighting for this nation; our nation, and we have as much right to it, and even more so, than most white people in this country. We helped make this country," the girl sitting in the back said with strong conviction in her words.

"And what's your name?" Jamison inquired.

"My name is Maria."

"What do the rest of you think about what Maria and Yousef had to say?"

Another student blurted out: "My uncle fought in Desert Storm."

"And your name?"

"My name is Bob or, I should say, Robert. It's one of those slave names if you believe what Yousef has to say."

"It is a slave name and the fact that you are proud of it tells me a lot about what you don't understand," Yousef shot back.

Jamison interrupted: "Let's have our discussion, but let's be civil with one another! Let's not be personal and attack each other. We want to share ideas. This is called learning. There is nothing wrong with having a difference of opinion in discussing controversial issues. War is controversial. War involves life and death and it is a matter we all need to take very seriously. So let's keep the disagreement respectful. Let's not personalize this and start attacking each other personally. We want to discuss the ideas. That's what this is really all about."

He was making clear the house rules and the parameters that must be respected if they were to carry on a civil discussion about these important issues.

"Mr. J, aren't you from Chicago? Did you know Milton Olive?" Shanekwa interjected.

Mr. Jamison was from Chicago. He did not know Milton Olive personally but he knew of him. Jamison informed the class and confirmed what Shanekwa thought might be the case. Jamison grew up on the west side of Chicago while Milton Olive grew up on the south side.

"Milton and I were about the same age," Jamison continued. "He went into the military about the same time that I went on to college. I would do everything in my power over the next years of my life to stay out of the military and to stay out of the war for which he was volunteering. How many of you have heard of the Vietnam War? I thought all of you had and I'm glad to see it has not been forgotten. For me back in the day, it was a very clear-cut issue in that I was opposed to going into Southeast Asia and fighting against people of color who were trying to throw off the yoke of colonialism."

"Amen to that. You may have a slave name but you know how to think," Yousef said with conviction.

"Thank you Mister Yousef," Jamison responded. Some chuckles were heard.

Jamison told the students about the difference in the environments Milton and he grew up in Chicago. Blacks on the south side, especially where Milton resided and further south, tended to be homeowners. Blacks on the west side tended by far to be apartment renters. There was always a schism in the Windy City between south side blacks and west side blacks. Those on the west side referred to the ones on the south side as the black bourgeoisie; while south side blacks tended to look down upon the west-siders as second-class. Jamison told the students about how indeed he was second-class and that he grew up in the Henry Horner housing projects while Milton and his family had a relatively nice house out south.

"I didn't know you lived in the jects, Mister J," Shanekwa said with affection in her voice and now knowing that one of her favorite teachers was from an environment very similar to her own. She lived in the low income housing there on Long Island and now felt a stronger affinity toward her teacher. She saw him as one of them more than ever before.

Jamison continued on, telling the students about the variety of jobs he did growing up. He had been a paperboy, he shined shoes downtown in Chicago, he worked in the Water Market, when it was on the west side of the city, unloading trucks, stacking crates and doing those kinds of odd jobs real early in the morning to make a few bucks before he went off to school. He pointed out that Milton Olive, to the best of his knowledge, did not do those kinds of jobs in Chicago. But he quickly added that it was probably because he was very small. Milton did some physical work around the farm when he was back in Lexington, Jamison reminded the students. No matter how small you are you could feed the chickens and collect the eggs.

Jamison attended Crane High School on the west side, a public high school with not exactly the best academic reputation in the world. Milton, on the other hand, went to a private Catholic school on the south side before later transferring to a public high school and then dropping out. He certainly had a chance for far superior education to the one that Jamison was afforded. Nevertheless, it was Jamison who went on to get his college degree at the University of Illinois in Urbana-Champaign in history and a Masters beyond that.

"I think the real thing is what it is you want to be," Jamison said to the students. "For me, I wanted more than anything else in the world to get an education and to be something other than another failed black kid, your typical product of the housing projects as everyone expected."

"Amen to that," Shanekwa added in. Laughter broke out in the class because many of the students were from backgrounds very similar to Shanekwa Lewis. In fact, one thing the students shared in common was that virtually all of them were from poor or working-class backgrounds. For them public housing was the norm rather than the exception.

Jamison used this opportunity to reinforce to them repeatedly that it was all about getting an education. "If I could get you to believe anything in the world, the one thing I would want you all to take to heart is that you can be what you want to be if you get an education. The key will not be for you young men in here how fast you can run a football, whether you can score a lot of points with a basketball. And you girls you have less opportunities than that. What I'm telling you is it's all about your brain. It's all about knowledge. Take advantage of these years here at the Milton Olive school and learn. Prepare yourselves for the next step. Prepare yourself for high school and to go beyond that. You have to have a college education in today's world or you have no future. It is not debatable. Education is the key."

"Well, it's too bad you didn't know Milton and you could've told him all of that back then rather than him going off to be in the white man's army," Yousef offered his assessment.

"But, Yousef, and all of you, it was a very different era back then. I'm a baby boomer. I was born after World War II and came of age in the 60s.   You've heard about that glorious, rambunctious, rebellious period, right? For all of us who came of age during that time -- you know we were folks who lived through the 50s and were raised as kids on Audie Murphy and John Wayne."

"Audie who and John what?" Several students murmured simultaneously.

Jamison had forgotten momentarily that his very young audience grew up in a much different world and he quickly was forced to remember that and took time to tell them briefly who was Audie Murphy and who was John Wayne. He explained to the students that Murphy was the most decorated American war hero in World War II, winning virtually every medal the military could confer including the Medal of Honor.

One student in the class was all smiles. It was Murphy who, as he whispered to those around him, let them know that he was named after Audie Murphy.

John Wayne, Jamison informed them, was a movie star who did many westerns that were hugely popular in the era. Wayne, "The Duke," he told them, was always the rugged tough guy, manly figure who was true grit and all about soaking it up and standing your ground. He shared with them that Wayne and Murphy were what he grew up on as did most baby-boomer males of that era whether black or white, Latino, Asian or anything else. You pretty much accepted that was the way men were supposed to be. They were expected to be providers, tough, manly, who would not retreat in the face of the enemy whether in the western or in the real world of war, with life-and-death on the line.

He tried to convey to them that was the world that shaped Milton Olive; that he grew up believing in and accepting as the way you were supposed to act as a real man. It was all about valor, toughness, and perseverance.

Jamison felt certain that the students could see his point and that they were starting to sense the dilemma for Milton who as a small and fragile individual may have been one who felt even more deeply than others the need to prove himself, to test his mettle, and despite his small size somehow demonstrate that he was a man's man in a world characterized by Audie Murphy and John Wayne.

"So for me, I went off to college in Urbana-Champaign and I was able to get a deferment because I was a student in college. The deferment kept me out of the war, a war which I thought was wrong, immoral, and I wanted no part of. It was no doubt my history education that helped me gain a certain perspective on Southeast Asia, Vietnam, and European colonialism. While I never demonstrated and was not involved in campus unrest as such, my heart was with the demonstrations; my heart was with those issues."

"But Mister Jamison how did you choose not to belong in the protests and those demonstrations and the rest? You told us that young Milton was involved in the civil rights movement in the South. Wasn't he more of a doer than you? Were you a coward? I mean, you didn't go fight in the war and you didn't fight for things here at home. Did you?"

"And your name?"

"I am Jesus Sanchez. My older brother fought in Iraq. He was wounded and won a Purple Heart.

He's home now. He says that he was fighting to make America safe. Maybe Milton Olive felt the same way."   Jesus made some strong points and solid observations, and Jamison acknowledged that and thanked him for his hard-hitting statement and question.

"You are right," Jamison said. "I should have been more involved. I should have participated in the civil rights movement. I should have been involved in the black student movement at the University of Illinois.   But I spent my time studying, trying to get good grades, trying to survive Urbana-Champaign and the tough and demanding academic work. Despite that, you are right. I should have done more and gone beyond just looking out for my future. I should have been an activist. But I was not. I didn't even play football and I am a pretty big guy."

The students all laughed at that last remark. It seemed clear too that the group appreciated his honesty about his own shortcomings. "Milton did what he thought was right and what he believed in. We need to respect that, right?" Jamison asked. The students nodded with approval for the most part. Yousef shook his head in a vote of a resounding no.

"He was wrong," Yousef said. "The young brother didn't know any better. He had not had a chance to read and learn or didn't bother to do it. I think his father was to blame. He should have been telling his son what it was like to be a black man in America. I think his father, senior, was part of the problem, and as brother Malcolm would say, 'You are either part of the solution or you are part of the problem.'"

"Do all of you know who Malcolm X. was?" Jamison asked the group. Only two blurted out in the affirmative.   Most had no knowledge of Malcolm X so he told them briefly about him, the Nation of Islam or so-called Black Muslims, and about its leader, Elijah Mohammad, and the philosophy of black separatism and self-reliance. Jamison well knew of the nation because Mosque Number II, the headquarters of the National of Islam, was there in his and Milton's hometown of Chicago.

Jamison got back to the focus of his recitation: Milton L. Olive, III. "Milton made his choice to the best of his ability at the time. That's what I think," Jamison told the students. "He was 17 years old when he decided that of the options his father gave him, he would join the military. Since he was not 18 yet, his father had to sign for him to authorize his induction into the army. And he did. Milton was on his way into the armed forces as the conflict in Vietnam was starting to heat up.

I doubt that he would have made a different choice even if he knew in advance that he would be called upon to fight. He was like many young enlistees in recent years that see the military as a career move, a place where you could be a part of something deemed honorable, get an education and learn a skill that prepares you later on for a good paying job. I doubt that most today knew that they would end up in a real shooting war in Iraq or Afghanistan or someplace like that."

There was still snow on the ground when Milton left home early that spring to report for induction. He joined not only the army but one of its most rugged divisions.

Chapter II:
Basics

Life is all about making decisions. You are born, you grow, and you mature. At every step of the way from being an infant to the most mature adult, it is all about decision-making. You have choices, or you try to have choices. You most certainly have decisions to make about what is right, what is wrong, what I will do, or what I will not do. For Milton he made a decision as he neared his 18th year of life, that he would join the United States Army.

Jamison pointed out: "Now I don't know if he made that decision because he bowed to the pressure from his father to do something. I think there was real pressure on him to do something because he was floundering about. Like many young people, just like many of you, you sometimes are not sure what you want to do. But at some point you will have to make a decision. For Milton he made it."

"Mister J," Shanekwa spoke, "I have heard the story before but I think my position about Milton has changed."

"How so?"

"I first thought that Milton made the right decision by choosing the military. I am starting to question whether that was the right decision maybe because I know what happened to him in the end. I think it's more that I just wanted him to have more options in his life. It seemed to me very unfair that someone that young had to make that tough of a choice and in the end made a decision that would cost him so much."

"Shanekwa you make a good point. I wish I could answer it for you. All I can tell you is that you, and the rest of the students here, will all have to make choices. Some of you made the choice today that you would fight and that of course was the wrong choice. You will be faced with choices all through life and you can't afford to make the wrong ones. I can't judge whether Milton's choice was right or wrong for him. It is not the choice I would have made but it was the choice he made. Please keep this in mind that as you grow older you will have to make important choices in life, many of them. It is time now to start making the right choices, the best decisions that you can possibly muster."

Students seemed generally moved by Jamison's urging. There was a long silence pause with no one saying a word, and the young minds clearly wrestling with what he said.

Alfred had been quiet until now: "I think it is wrong to take a life under any circumstances.

Fighting is crazy too. I am in this room because I was trying to break up the fight that my friends were starting in the hall. No one listens to me. I think people, humans, have a thing about killing, about fighting, about war. We should practice war no more, is what I have been taught by my mother and father."

"Comments about Alfred's point? It's an important one. What do you think about killing, about war? Should violence be avoided at all times or is there a time and place for it?" Jamison wondered out loud.

"You have to be willing to fight for what is right," Murphy told the group.

"Yeah, but was Vietnam right?" Alfred retorted. "That's why I say not to fight no matter what. You don't have to worry about fighting for the wrong cause if you don't believe in fighting. Settle it with talk, like we are trying to do here."

There was a long silence in the classroom. You could see that many of the students did not agree with Alfred yet they were not willing to raise counterpoints, with the exception of Murphy.

The focus went back to Milton. He signed on the dotted line and could not change his mind and refuse induction. Whether he would have to fight or not was a moot question. He had made up his mind, and he was going on to a new adventure.

Spring was on the horizon after a rough Chicago winter. Milton was eager to report to begin basic training. One can only know whether the Chicago harsh winds, and being tucked away in their house there on the south side, may have been factors in his decision. Maybe not. He was going to get out of the house for sure and he would very soon be in a warmer climate, although that had little to do with his decision to join the military. Chicago's winters were rough but not so rough that they would force you to make a career choice that ultimately involved or potentially involved taking of life.

Two days before he was scheduled to report for induction, he and his father and stepmother enjoyed a nice home-cooked meal together, just the three of them. There was not a lot said. Milton was in a contemplative mood as was his father and stepmother. They dined on his favorite which was turkey with all the trimmings although it was not Thanksgiving. Nevertheless, stepmom Antoinette took it upon herself to make the huge family meal.

Only on occasion during the dinner would Milton's father do more than just stare at his son and actually say something.

"I think you've made the right decision," Olive senior would say from time to time. "You could still go back to school if you want. Although I know you don't like the prospects of you losing the year since all the credits from school in the South don't seem to be accepted by the school up here. Keep in mind son, you have plenty of time and losing the year is really not much."

The fact of the matter was that young Milton was committed to his decision. Neither did he want to change his mind. Plus he was not interested at all in attending public school in Chicago. His father in their discussions had made it clear to him that given the financial constraints, and Milton's lackluster approach to schooling, that he was going to have to continue at Englewood Public High School rather than the costly private parochial school. That was likely a factor in young Milton's mine although he did not like the private school very much either. He had no desire for more formal education and that was the bottom line. He had made his decision.

A few days later at the crack of dawn he was up, dressed and ready to go out the door, with his father volunteering to drive him to the train station. Milton repeated several times that he called a cab and there was no need for his father to drive him. On further thought, he decided to cancel the taxi and to have one more opportunity to chat with his dad, in this case on the drive to the train station.

Instead of many words being exchanged during the drive, there was an eerie quiet between the two men. As they neared the Illinois Central Railroad station, Olive senior gave his son one final word of advice:

"Take care of yourself. Do your job. Make the most of the opportunity. Make us proud of you."

Milton replied, "Thanks Dad. I promise not to let you down. I know I've not been the greatest son in the world. Here's my chance to prove myself and get going in the right direction. I plan to make you all proud." Looking back in hindsight, Milton's words were prophetic to say the least.

This was the first time young Milton was going to somewhere other than Mississippi. He was traveling down South but in a different direction. His orders called for him to report to the United States Army Base in Fort Benning, Georgia. He would be there the next morning and ready to experience military life and a new world of what he hoped would be adventure and personal fulfillment. For now, he could sit back and enjoy the eight hundred mile train ride and the passage of scenery as he moved from Illinois southeast to his rendezvous with destiny.

Milton thought of what military life might be like. It would be a good proving ground for him to show people that he was much stronger than his small frame might indicate. His mind was made up that he would be an outstanding soldier. He looked forward to the discipline and structured way of life that the military would afford him. He also appreciated that this would be the first time ever that he was not under the thumb of either his parents or grandparents. He was, in the most practical sense of the term, a grown man, and he liked the idea. He thought about where he could go and what he could do. This was intriguing to Milton as it would be for any young person on their own for the first time. He was stepping out and into the world where he would be his own man's man.

He continued to talk to himself until he drifted off to sleep. He was surprised when he awakened and looked out of his window and no longer saw snowcapped scenery. Instead, there was greenery. Then he heard the conductor calling out "Fort Benning!" He was arriving, and arriving at more than just the idea of coming to a physical place; he was arriving at the opportunity he had afforded himself to become an adult, to make his own way in the world, and to make a difference. He promised himself again that he was going to be a superb soldier, a great one.

The train virtually deposited him at the doorstep of Fort Benning. He had taken the physical and the intelligence tests back in Chicago where he signed up. It was now going to be about proving himself mentally and physically in the real and demanding military world.

Milton immediately liked what was before him. He saw a nice structured compound as far as one could see. There were gates and the place was confined behind walls and bobbed wire. There were military checkpoints and as he walked, carrying his suitcase to the front gate, he noticed that he was no longer alone and at least fifteen or twenty other young men were with him who must have been on the same train.

They were recent inductees just like himself and they came from a variety of places. Not all of them got on the train at Chicago; it made a number of other stops. Neither were they all black or white. There were some Hispanics and he thought a couple of Asians. What was clear to anyone was that they were all Americans.

The signs indicated everything very clearly and if you somehow missed them you heard the MPs at the gates at the front of the compound making it very clear that you were to report to station A, and that was ahead of you about two hundred yards in the huge building that looked like a warehouse.

There was a trim and fit looking sergeant standing directly in front of the door and telling the new enlistees that they were not fit to come in to the premises yet and needed to form straight lines and columns of twelve each facing the facility. Milton and the others eagerly complied.

"I'm not going to yell and scream as you have seen sergeants do in the John Wayne movies. It is not like that in this man's army. I shall speak with a clear voice and one that you can easily understand. I don't like to yell. Please don't make me yell. The consequences will be too grave. I am here to turn you plebs into soldiers. I'm here to make you into fighting men. If you follow my orders, my directions, you will learn, you will become fighting men, and you will prevail. I am in the business of creating tough guys. If you are a pussy, you are in the wrong place! If you are a sissy, you are in the wrong place! If you are white, Negro, Mexican, or one of those other groups, you are in the wrong place! We train American fighting men. That's the only race of men we're interested in. This is Fort Benning. We train the best to be the best. I am Sergeant Kyle and for the next six weeks of your basic training I am your mother, your father, your priest, your Rabbi, your best friend and your worst enemy, if you foul up! Don't screw up! We will make you into U. S. Army grunts. That is one of the finest words and categories in the American language, a grunt. It means that you hump and carry your own weight as an American fighting man. You are not fit at this point to be grunts but I will make you into them. So grab your gear and give your information to the listing clerk and report to your assigned barracks for further instructions. That is all. Dismissed!"

Kyle's words rung loud and clear for Milton, even though the sergeant really did not yell and scream. He spoke in a very deliberate and well-enunciated voice. It was a voice of authority. It was the voice of the person who was going to train you and make you into a soldier, and that was what Milton wanted. He figured that if he could make it under Kyle's watchful eye, it would prove to everyone back home and to himself that he was a real man.

After the orientation talk from the sergeant he and the others signed some paperwork, including insurance policies. Milton designated that the payments would go to his father if he were killed in action. That was the last thing on his mind as he went over to the PX and lined up for the issuance of uniforms. The soldiers working performed their duties like a well-oiled machine. They did not even ask Milton what was his height or weight. One of them just glanced at him and then yelled over to the other who was behind the equipment cage "smalls." He was saying, in no uncertain terms, that this enlisted man was small in stature. He was asked a question by one of the soldiers handing out equipment: What was his shoe size? They did ask for that. Just like the rest of him, Milton's feet were small. He wore a size seven and a half.

With equipment in hand he headed back to the barracks to get dressed. He looked to the other men to see exactly how they were putting on their uniform because he was not sure, although he knew where shirts and pants went of course but not much beyond that. Trying hard, he got it all done rather quickly and in good form. Venturing into the latrine, he asked one of the other soldiers if he had a mirror. The answer was no. The other soldier was willing to look him over and tell him if his uniform was on correctly. The army liked the idea of one man helping another. This was the military and not a department store. There were no mirrors for one to view himself. The comrade told Milton that everything was "A-okay." Milton returned the inspection favor in kind, giving his fellow soldier a thumps up.

Milton looked fit and snappy in his uniform. He was a soldier now for real. The uniform did not lie. To say that he was proud of his uniform would be like saying that the face of the sun is somewhat hot. He was ecstatic about how he looked and could not hold back the giant smile on his face.

They were instructed that at 18 hundred hours sharp they were due to be at the dining hall for chow. He wanted to make sure that he was there on time because they were also told that fighting men did not spend a lot of time eating. You wanted to be on time because you would not have more than a total of thirty minutes to get your food and to finish eating. They were letting you know in no uncertain terms that you were on army time now.

Milton loved every moment of it. To him this was a new adventure, an opportunity to bond with himself and with others. He occasionally struck up conversations with his fellow GIs. Milton had never been one to take the first step in introducing himself or saying hello to folks when he was in Chicago or for that matter in Lexington. At Fort Benning he did it. He was coming into his own and quickly. Milton asked the person in front of him and the one behind him in the chow line where they hailed from. He felt that he was among a band of brothers, what the army wanted him to feel.

What amazed him was that the food was actually very good. He had heard stories about army food, G.I. rations, powdered eggs, and all of those other accounts about how uninviting and tasteless were the meals in the military. He immediately found that to be untrue. The meal that evening featured steak, potatoes, green beans, and some sort of gravy, along with biscuits, milk, orange juice, and Coca-Cola if you so desired. He really enjoyed his meal and there was a lot of upbeat chatter. He thought that maybe one of the sergeants would yell out to keep it quiet. That was not the case. The men chatted away as if at a family meal and having a joyous time together.

When full, he cleaned his dishes and stacked his tray the same as those in front of him did and went back to the barracks thinking that he would take it easy. He was right that there was nothing else on the agenda for that evening. Milton took the free time and roamed around Fort Benning getting to know his environment. He knew however that, as he had been told and warned, they would all go to work in the most serious fashion early tomorrow morning.

Milton did not sleep that well the first night at the base. No doubt part of the reason was the unfamiliar setting. The cot he laid on was comfortable though nowhere as nice as his bed back in Chicago or when he visited his grandparents in Lexington. What dominated his thoughts were the changes in his life, where he was now, what was being expected of him, and what tomorrow might bring.

He eventually drifted off into a shallow sleep only to be rudely awakened a few hours later by the blasting sound of trumpets over the amplification system. It was revelry, the call to get up. The sergeant was walking through the barracks and instructing them to "rise and shine" and take no more than fifteen minutes to clean up, brush their teeth, get dressed, and to assemble in front of the barracks. When Milton finally did note the time on his G.I. issued watch, he saw that it was the ungodly hour of 4 a.m. or 04 hundred hours military time. He was in the army now.

It was a strange experience for him to be in the latrine area with its rows of urinals and across the way the equal number of rows of toilets. On the other side were a massive row of sinks and a huge shower stall with what seemed like endless rows of shower heads. Some men were taking showers or using the john and that too was a public affair. It was uncomfortable at first for Milton to be washing up and using the toilet in front of a group of complete strangers. After all, he had been an only child and was used to complete privacy when using the bathroom.

Those days were over. Also, most of the men were shaving. Not Milton. He had no facial hairs yet and there was no need of him to try and fake it. He washed, put on his deodorant, and brushed his teeth really well as he always did. When he looked for a cup to rinse out his mouth, he was surprised to find that the army did not provide any. You cupped your palms and held them under the running water from the faucet, then slurped the water from your hands, gargled and spit it out. It was efficient although something to which Milton was certainly not accustomed. He would get used to it. As he told himself, "You're in the army now."

"All of that is not very pleasant," one of the girls in the class blurted out.

The boys likewise murmured in agreement.

Jamison informed them: "Well, Milton was in the army and had to learn to adjust. We all have to learn to adjust to things, right?"

There were chuckles, smiles, and some laughter from the students and then one of them spoke out: "But going to the toilet with everyone watching is not something I would want to adjust too!"

The entire class broke into laughter for a good thirty seconds or more before Jamison returned to telling Milton's story.

Milton dressed in a hurry in his fatigues and rushed out with others in front of the barracks and lined up according to height as ordered. He was ready for the day's work to begin, he and the forty-plus other men of his unit. Sergeant Kyle positioned himself front and center of the four lines of the group of soldiers and barked out

"Attent-huh!" The group came smartly to attention including Milton who had never done this before but based on all of the war movies he had seen knew that you were supposed to come sharply to order. He and the others stood straight with heels together and looking straightforward with hands at the seams of the trousers. Almost all of the men got it right without any instruction.

Even Sergeant Kyle was impressed. He then yelled out "Dress right, dress!" And the men executed it extremely well, which was with the right hand still at the seams of the trousers, the left arm was extended outward to the left and the head turned sharply to the right. When the appropriate distance was achieved between soldiers, the sergeant commanded: "Ready, front!" To which all arms came smartly down and the individual's head snapping back sharply straightforward. Milton caught on quickly. He enjoyed it.

Sergeant Kyle did not waste time showing his unit how to do a left face or right face or about face. He simply called out these commands and it was done properly by most of the men, to which Kyle said, "Outstanding! Now let's get it perfect." The other NCOs (non-commissioned officers) walking amongst the group were most helpful in demonstrating from time to time the proper way to get it done. The unit caught on quickly and after another thirty minutes or so of trial and error and more "forward march and to-the-rear march" they had it down pat. They might not have been as precise as a seasoned group, but they were pretty darn good. In another half an hour or so of drilling the unit could perform all of the basic maneuvers quite satisfactorily.

The unit looked good as it marched along in straight columns and in step with Sergeant Kyle barking out an occasional "left, right, left" and "hup, two, three, four, hup, two three four!" It was fun to Milton. He loved the precision of it all and the feeling of being part of a group.

After about two hours of the marching and the repeated commands, Sergeant Kyle called the group to "halt" and ordered "at ease." He told them that he was relatively impressed with their performance and thus was going to dismiss them so that they could go and have some breakfast, some chow, at 07 hundred hours. Kyle also told the men -- tongue-in-cheek -- that after chow they could relax, play baseball or touch football, watch some TV, or do whatever they wanted to do because they would be back on the field after that in full gear and required to do some "real work." With that, Kyle dismissed the unit.

Some of the men started running toward the mess hall knowing that they did not have much time to both eat, have a few minutes to relax, and then to get ready with full backpacks and be back on the field. Some went to the john in between all of this and you certainly did not have much time there either. It was the army and not a fancy social club. Milton still found it to be almost fun and games at this point. He ran with the rest to the mess hall and had a nice chow-down of breakfast which consisted of eggs, (whether they were powdered or not is debatable), bacon, sausage, grits (after all they were in the South), toasted bread with jam on the side, and choices of coffee, milk, orange juice, and water.

Some of the soldiers focused on certain items in particular. Back then, you did have a choice when you came up to the mess hall attendees who were dishing out the grub. Certainly you had a choice when it came to what you wanted to drink. Many of the soldiers took glasses of every beverage. Others simply liked as much coffee as they could get while others, and most of them, went for orange juice as the beverage of choice. Very few took milk. It was probably not so much that they disliked milk than the image they might think it gave to their fellow unit members if they were seen drinking it. Real men, of course, did not drink milk -- some wanted to convey; Milton among them. He loved milk but passed on drinking it in the army.

Milton quickly finished his food and made it back to the barracks. There were the NCOs walking about instructing the men on packing their gear into the field packs that were laid out at the foot of each bunk. In less than fifteen minutes the men had all items packed as prescribed. In full fatigues and with backpacks on, they were all back on the field and ready to go.

Sergeant Kyle appeared. He was also in full gear and with a backpack. He then informed his trainees that they were about to take a "little walk" on a beautiful morning in the South. He was being facetious, of course, and everyone knew it. The sergeant ordered the company to attention and then commanded "right face" and "forward march." He kept the march at a lively pace all the way to the southern tip of Fort Benning, a huge army facility going many miles in every conceivable direction. That morning, the unit was going to get to know a sizable chunk of it.

The marching lasted for precisely one hour and then the sergeant in a sarcastic voice asked the group, "Would you ladies like to take a rest now?" No one dared answer. The sergeant of course did not mean it. He then ordered "At the quickstep, march." This meant to quicken the pace almost to a jog. The unit, including Milton, was starting to tire from the pace after about twenty minutes. Rather than slowing, Sergeant Kyle announced that it was time to take "a nice little run." He ordered the group to move it "on the run!" They were jogging now. It was not at the fastest pace but it was far quicker than anything previous. The backpacks felt heavier than ever. After only ten minutes at the run, heavy breathing could be heard throughout the ranks.

Milton among them. His backpack felt like it weighed a ton, even though it actually weighted twenty-five pounds. The weight would increase as the training increased in later days. But for now it was far more than enough and after a few more minutes one could hear the gasping for air by virtually everyone in the unit. They were not in as good shape as they thought, as the sergeant was showing them. After about a mile at that pace, the sergeant slowed it back to the "quick pace."

At least they were back to walking again even at the lively cadence. Then the sergeant slowed it down a bit more, saying to the group, "I'm glad you are enjoying our little walk." He was letting the unit cool down before he mercifully raised his right hand and commanded "halt! Take five!"

Everyone was delighted to hear those magical words. Some of the men fell to their knees, others just laid out flat, while others bent over puking their guts out at this first day of serious training.

Milton could not believe how tough it had been marching and running the distance the sergeant prescribed. He also realized that the unit was far from its starting point and that they would have to make it all the way back. In short, if they turned around right now they would have the same distance in their return route. The army was becoming a little less fun to Milton at this moment. He saw that this was tough work and with more to come. At the same time he said to himself: "This is what it's about. I can do this. I'll show them."

After a few minutes rest and the opportunity to take in a drink of water from their canteens, the unit was ready for the long return trip. They had gone a long distance and at least they would be back at the base and to a degree of comfort in a couple of hours. No such luck. Kyle had something else in store for them. When he called the unit to order, he said to them: "Let's enjoy our walk a little more. The unit moved out, continuing in the same direction away from the center of the base. They marched for another five miles before the sergeant said, "Let's go home."

The unit turned about and started the long march home. They had gone ten miles in one direction. There was a lot of grumbling amongst the troop to which Kyle immediately heard and said to them "I don't want to hear that crap! Stop your crying. You're in the army now! And since you have the strength to grumble then you have the strength to speed it up." He ordered "At the quick step!" The unit sped up its pace and kept it up for the next mile before the sergeant slowed it down.

They hiked for another two straight hours without stopping for a rest. A number of members of the unit began puking on themselves. Others began to moan out loud that this was killing them. They should have known better. When the sergeant heard the complaining he sped up the march again. After a mile or two more, some soldiers were saying to others that somebody needed to say something to the sergeant "before he kills all of us." No one dared.

It would have done no good and may have made things even worse. The sergeant knew exactly what he was doing and there was no thought whatsoever of making it any easier on the troopers. They were not the first group of men he had trained in his long career.

After another three or four miles, the sergeant mercifully called halt and gave the men a five minute rest. Some fell to their knees; some laid out on their backs and others on their stomachs. They were spent.

While they huffed and puffed, he strolled up and down the ranks preaching to them: "You wanted to be in the army. You're in it. You've got to be in shape. There is no time to rest when you're in the field, when you are in battle. What do you think the enemy will be doing when you're lounging about taking a siesta? You got to be ready and able to fight at all times. You volunteered to be in my army, didn't you? Don't answer that. You are all volunteers. You can volunteer to get out of my army as easy as you said you wanted to be in. I don't want to hear any more complaints. This is the U.S. Army. It's all about being tough, being ready, being able, and always, I mean always, ready to fight and defend the United States of America. If that is not what you're up to, get out of my beloved army!"

He also informed the men that he wanted to make it back to camp in far less time than it took them to reach the present point. In short, they would be doing a combination of quick stepping, and jogging, with only slight intervals of rest in between. This was a pace that was sure to have many fall by the wayside or prove that they had all the right stuff. The sergeant knew this very well. He hesitated only for a moment to encourage his unit with, "If you are going to be able to survive in combat, you must be in fighting shape. You have got to be fighting ready. This is no fun and games. You are American GIs. Up on your feet. Let's go home!"

The moans and groans stopped for good. The sergeant ordered the men to move out. "You're going to love this," and with that he commanded, "At the quick pace!" The unit moved out briskly and without a word. When Kyle finally did call them to a halt and a brief rest, almost half the unit was puking up its guts.

Milton was among them and beginning to rethink his commitment to the military and starting to wonder how he got himself into this situation. He told himself that he was just a teenager and did not know for sure what he wanted to do. He was having serious second thoughts about his choice. Yes, he told himself that he decided on the military. However, he did not want to kill himself. At no time did Milton think that by joining the army it meant that he would have to forfeit his life. He wanted to survive just like everyone else. He had seen his share of John Wayne movies and never thought of himself as the one coming home in a coffin with the American flag draped over it. If anything, he thought of himself as the hero, who survived the onslaught and brought everyone else and himself back safely.

The rigors of the field exercise had him questioning everything. If this was the physical price you paid in terms of this kind of training, he wondered aloud whether he could do it. This, after all, was only the unit's first outing. He asked himself in all earnestness: "What will the next one, and the one after that, and the one after that be like?"

He realized that it was already a make-it or break-it moment for him. Milton talked to himself in earnest about his stamina and personal desire to achieve. He started challenging himself with his own words and remembering that he had promised to make it. Sure he was dead tired just like everyone else in the unit. At the same time he told himself, "I can make it. I have to make. I will make it."

The unit alternated from quick pace, to jog, to walk, and then started all over again. The sergeant conveniently forgot about having the men take additional periodic respites on the return march. It seemed like an eternity for the unit to make it back to the base. They were sweaty, dog tired, smelly, angry, thirsty, and frustrated. They were all the things that Sergeant Kyle wanted them to be, wanted them to feel. He was a veteran of World War II. He had been part of the expeditionary forces that landed on Saipan. He not only had a Purple Heart for being wounded in battle, but he was a proud recipient of the Bronze Star. Yes, Kyle was your quintessential battle-tested sergeant, in addition to being a hero. He was made of all the right stuff. And he expected no less from each and every one of his men. His job, as he saw it, as the army told him as well, was to get them ready to fight, to kill, and to survive. He was imminently able and committed to that task.

Some three hours later, the unit finally made it back to the base. Milton did not even take a shower that evening despite the rigorous outing, the sweating, the stench, and the trials and tribulations of it all. He was just too doggone tired to take a shower and hit the bunk in full dress and immediately fell sound asleep. If he had noticed, he would have seen that he was not the only one who collapsed to their bunk from exhaustion. He slept through the evening meal, too tired to eat or even think about food.

He woke the next morning at about 03 hundred hours, an hour before revelry. He sat on the end of his bunk listening to the snoring of his unit members and thinking to himself if he had made the right decision. In those questions to himself and answers that he inevitably gave, Milton L. Olive, III, despite his age, concluded that he knew himself and what he wanted to achieve and that he was dedicated to being not just a good soldier but the best soldier in the U.S. Army. He may not have amounted to much in other circumstances, he admitted to himself. This would be his chance. Milton knew he had never been a great student, to say the least. He also knew that he disappointed his father by not excelling in academics or wanting to go on to higher education. The U.S.

Army was his home and his ladder up. He was going to show all who cared and all who doubted, that Milton Olive was somebody and could excel at this, the most rigorous test of manhood imaginable. He made an irreversible commitment to himself that early morning that he would rather die than fail in his effort to become a U. S. soldier.

Milton's early rise afforded him virtual private use of the latrine that morning. He gathered his toiletries and hit the showers. If it had been full of his fellow soldiers, he still would have taken the shower that he desperately needed. He took off his skivvies and embraced the flow of water like never before as he washed his head and the rest of his body and quenched himself in the embrace of a thorough cleaning. It felt so incredibly good.

After drying off and brushing his teeth, he put on his deodorant and a clean pair of skivvies. It was not quite 04 hundred hours and he knew that revelry would be sounded loud and clear at any moment. Milton felt pumped up as if he had drunk a whole pot of coffee and decided that he would get fully dressed now and be the first on the field. He put on the set of clean fatigues that were in his footlocker, a clean pair of socks, everything. He was ready.

When revelry sounded, Milton was already standing on the field awaiting everyone else to awaken, get dressed, and to join him. Sergeant Kyle showed up even earlier than usual and peeped into the quarters before he noted that one unit member was already standing on the field in full fatigues and ready to go. In that one moment, Milton won the respect of Sergeant Kyle. The sergeant knew that he had an eager beaver and someone dedicated to the cause. Kyle gave a half smile to Milton before he turned and entered the quarters to make his presence known.

The maneuvers that morning were short and to the point. Sergeant Kyle thanked the men for joining him in what he called the walk in the park yesterday. He told the men that what they had experienced was a demonstration that they were not yet soldiers, not yet in shape. They needed a lot of work and most of all to get in military condition. Kyle made it clear that conditioning would be his emphasis for the next weeks of basic training. He wanted them to run to every place including to chow, the latrine, and the commissary – every place. The sergeant told them if he found any man walking from one locale to another and taking his time, that there would be hell to pay. He then urged the men to enjoy their breakfast, and then after eating to meet him on the field in full gear with backpacks. They were going to take another little stroll.

The men were soon gathered after chow and ready to go or, as the sergeant liked to way, "ready to jump off." He called them to attention, then to a right face, followed by move it out at the quickstep. The unit kept marching at the quick pace for a good two or three miles before the sergeant gave them a break. Mercifully, after a ten minute pause, Kyle turned the group around and headed them back to base. Once back they were allowed a break and to prepare for more maneuvers later that afternoon.

The next of the maneuvers as such was a trip to the rifle range. It was there that Milton learned how to shoot and the proper way to handle his M-14. He never fired a weapon before even when he was in Mississippi on the farm. This was a new and, at first, frightening experience for him.

Yet he caught on rather quickly and settled into being a fairly decent marksman.

All the procedures, drills, and exercises – – and there were days full of calisthenics – – were repeated every day except Sunday. Milton was being molded into what he signed on to be: a fighting machine. The exercises were fraught with the constant array of push-ups, sit-ups, and pull-ups. He was getting into shape and they sure were not wasting time. He and the others of his class had only six weeks to learn the basics.

Whether in rain or darkness of night, the training was relentless over those six weeks. Milton held his own throughout the ordeal. He was not exaggerating when he wrote home to relatives and friends that he was doing fine in the army. He wrote to one of his cousins that he might make the military his career and stay in it for the duration. He hoped to work himself up the ranks. Milton was catching the spirit of what the training at Fort Benning hoped to instill. Milton Olive was proud to wear the uniform of the United States Army.

The six weeks finally came to an end. Most in the unit had made it. This called for celebration. Fort Benning, during those years, did not have a formal graduation as such. It did, however, acknowledge at a major roll-call that the enlistees had completed their basic training and were now full-fledged soldiers. In celebration, they were given a seven-day pass to go home and be with family and friends. Everyone knew what this meant. It meant that when you returned you would receive your military assignment, and with the war in Vietnam starting to crank up, it seemed most likely that the assignment would be Southeast Asia. For the time being there was the opportunity to go home and to enjoy, and Milton reveled in the idea of doing so.

He and his cousin Charles, who also enlisted and completed the basic training at the fort, took the train ride back home together. They were two proud peacocks, glad to be wearing the uniforms of the United States Army. Milton's pride in his uniform was unabashed.

"You know we sometimes overlook the power of the uniform," Jamison directed his remarks to the students.

"What do you mean Mister Jamison?"

"What is your name," Jamison inquired of the inquisitive student. The student fumbled a bit before answering.

"My name is Sherry Combs."

"Thank you Sherry. Have you all noticed how important an individual seems to be when they have on a uniform? What about the police man or woman? Have any of you worn a uniform for some purpose?"

No hands went up, indicating that none of the students had ever worn a uniform of any sort or were not interested in answering the question. Jamison then asked if any of the students worked after school.

Two raised their hands. Both worked at a fast-food restaurant. The two students quickly acknowledged that they wore uniforms at work.

Jamison asked them what they thought was the purpose of the uniform.

Sherry was the only one to answer. "I think the customers probably like it. They know you work there. Maybe it makes you feel like you are part of a team. I guess that is what Milton probably felt; that he belonged to something; that he was a member."

"Exactly. That's precisely it," Jamison told the group. "The uniform indicates that you are a member of the team, that you are something special, that you have a group behind you. You belong. You are a member of a certain club, or fraternity or sorority, you're a person who has friends, associates, others who you fit in with."

The uniform made a powerful difference for young Milton. His military uniform made him stand out. He was somebody. In uniform, Milton was someone who mattered. He was a member of the United States Army, and proud of it.

When he and his cousin arrived back home everyone seeing them commented on how snappy and sharp they looked in their uniforms. Both were dressed, as the old-timers used to say, "To the nines." Pants were pressed with sharp creases in them. The shirts were freshly laundered with stiff, starched collars. The ties they wore matched up with the rest of their uniform in coordinated army khaki with the jacket. It was clear to anyone close or far away that these young men belonged. These young men were part of the army.

Cousin Charles, however, at the moment he got home he took off his uniform and went out that evening as a civilian and blended in with the bar scene. Milton kept his uniform on even when he was in the house. When he went out he wore his uniform. He was too young to make the bar scene. Nowhere near 21, he could not legally buy a drink, go into a nightclub, or vote. Yet he was in the army and could kill or die for his country.

"You know, Mister Jamison, that really sucks. I mean it's really unfair. They expect someone to go into the army and risk their lives but they can't even buy a drink. Isn't that crazy?" Shanekwa said.

"I see your point," Jamison replied. "What do others think?"

"The brother was lost and confused," was Yousef's assessment. "There he was all decked out in the white man's uniform, ready to fight, kill, or even die for this country, yet he couldn't buy himself a glass of beer or a shot of whiskey, which he should not have done anyhow, but I'm simply saying that he should have had that right to do so. That's what's crazy about this place. America is nuts. Go fight, go die, but you can't vote, you can't have a glass of beer. There's something basically wrong with that."

"I feel you, Yousef," Jamison responded. The class broke out in laughter since Jamison tried to be hip and use the lingo of the streets by telling Yousef that "I feel you." Jamison laughed too.

"Do others agree with Yousef?" Jamison inquired.

"I think Yousef has a point," Shanekwa stated.

"What do others think? Let's hear from some of the rest of you who we have not heard from," Jamison prodded. He was doing his best to get the whole group involved in the discussion but except for the three or four in particular, the rest seemed unwilling to engage in open discussion of the issues.

"Well, really, what do you think Mister J," Shanekwa wanted to hear Jamison's answer.

"I think it was and is terribly unfair," Jamison concurred.

No matter what anyone else may have thought in the group of students under Jamison's watch, or the black community of Chicago, his family, or people he passed in the street, the most important question was what Milton thought or felt. Every indication was that he did not yearn for a drink or an evening in a nightclub. Perhaps he wanted the franchise, the right to vote. For now he was just proud of himself and of his uniform.

One can raise the question about his level of consciousness and education and whether he fully thought through what all of this meant. It would likewise be unfair to hold a teenager to such a lofty standard or even hope or expect that one at the tender age of 17 or 18 to already have figured out the complexities of life well enough to see beyond the trappings of uniform or hoopla or what others might think. Milton was still a very young person trying to find his way in life and to establish who he was, not only for himself but for those around him. He was doing his best to define himself and his place in society; a society that demanded that you either declare yourself and make something of your life or, by default, exist at a substandard level with the lack of respect that comes with it.

Milton wanted to be somebody and in the United States Army with his uniform on, for him, he was starting to make his mark. Those who knew Milton commented on how he wore his uniform at all times around the house and when he ventured out to go for a walk or to the movies. The only time he did not ware it was when he went to bed. Milton kept his uniform in pristine shape and condition by ironing out any wrinkles that he might have acquired during the previous day of wearing, washing and ironing his shirt, and keeping his shoes spit-shined.

For the seven days that Milton was at home in Chicago he did not vary his routine much. He was up early. His stepmother was usually up early too and made breakfast for the family before she went off to teach school. The breakfasts were nice but not at his request. Milton was fully capable and ready to make his own breakfast and liked doing so, but Antoinette enjoyed doing it for her stepson.

After breakfast, Milton typically left the house by about 7 a.m. and would walk several miles keeping himself in shape and enjoying the unencumbered freedom before having to return to the base. On other days either early in the morning or sometime midday, he would walk over to the express way and take the el (the name given the elevated electric commuter trains of Chicago) north toward downtown, typically getting off near Taylor Street and walking three blocks over to Halstead. There he could browse in the Maxwell Street shopping area, what black Chicagoans referred to as 'Jew town,' and find bargains. He seldom bought any clothing but he liked the routine. He enjoyed walking amongst the people. He, of course, was always in his uniform and showing that off.

If he had one specific destination at all in the Maxwell Street area, it was to Jim's. Jim's World-Famous was known far and wide for the best polish-sausage in America. They were cooked and stacked right there on an open grille. Add a bun with plenty of mustard and grilled onions, and Milton was all set. He loved the sausage along with his favorite grape soda pop. Despite the sloppiness of Jim's famous sausage, Milton never got anything on his uniform. He ate slightly bent forward with his hands extended outward as far away from his body as possible making sure nothing dropped on his uniform.

He sometimes stopped at the no-name record shop there on Maxwell Street to see and hear the latest 45 rpm records, the most recent Motown cuts and Chi-town and Memphis hits, and other soul tunes. There was always the blues blasting down Halstead. This was the street, the area, that back in the 1940s and 1950s, gave the world Muddy Waters, Howlin' Wolf, John Lee Hooker, Coco Taylor, among others. Milton loved the music although he was not one to collect many records. He did have a few.

After getting his fill of the sights and sounds, smells and tastes of Maxwell Street, he on occasion ventured to one of the downtown movie theaters to catch a film for a couple of hours. He enjoyed getting popcorn and a bit more to eat. For such a little guy he could pack it away. Despite that, he still never gained much weight.

There were times that he walked over to Lake Michigan. He enjoyed the park there and watching the luxury yachts and sailboats along the lake front. Milton also liked that people took notice of him in his uniform. He always made sure he walked with his head held high and in good-posture military form. He was strutting.

Some days Milton just sat on one of the benches there in the lake front park, marveling at the water and looking at the beautiful Chicago skyline. He knew a little about the history of the great skyscrapers and the great architects such as William Jenney, the father of skyscrapers, Louis Sullivan and others. He knew of Frank Lloyd Wright and some of his creations that anyone was free to go and marvel at downtown and in Oak Park, west of Chicago.

Then there was the nice el-train ride back to his house on the south side. On more than one occasion he either set next to someone or someone came in and set next to him and struck up a conversation. They asked him about being in the military and he told them with great pride that he was doing his duty and serving his country. Milton had no problem at all talking about that aspect of his life. Where he fell short was when asked about more general topics such as "Are you a White Sox or Cubs fan?" Milton never paid much attention to baseball. He knew, of course of the two Chicago teams and, if he cared to, could declare himself for one or the other team so he would not seem out of touch with sports.

There was the occasion when a fellow G.I. set next to him on the ride home on the el and struck up a conversation about football. He asked Milton what he thought about the Bears that year with their sensational rookie halfback Gale Sayers. It was 1965 and Sayers was burning up the turf with dashing runs that brought the fans at Soldiers' Field Stadium to their feet time and again. Milton knew about Sayers and could at least say that he thought he was great. In truth, he had never been to a football game nor been to see the Chicago Bulls basketball team play. He and his father went to a Cubs baseball game one time and thus he knew of the African-American star player for the team, Ernie Banks. Milton was simply not a sports person.

One might have thought that Milton would have spent his time at the Field Museum of Natural History or the Museum of Science and Industry, two world-class museums right there in his city, but he did not. His father took him to both museums when he was around 9 or 10 years old, and he enjoyed the sights and sounds and the marvels that he saw. He liked the science museum much more than the natural history museum because it had some rides that you could try, going through a coal mine that they had there. In particular he enjoyed walking through the German submarine that was on display, the U-505 that was captured off the coast of West Africa on 4 June 1944 during the battle for the Atlantic in

World War II. The other museum, the Field Museum, was much more about ancient history and Milton did not find that of interest and stayed away from it.

As Jamison told that story, the class laughed rather loudly, since he was a history teacher. He knew what they were laughing about and he chuckled along with them for a bit.

All too quickly, the seven-day furlough at home came to an end and it was time to report back to Fort Benning. Milton felt sad to some extent about leaving his family. On the other hand, he actually enjoyed the military and was in a sense eager to get back. Also, he had made the decision that he now shared with his father. He told his dad that while basic training had officially come to an end, and he was celebrating that, he made a decision to put his name forward for advanced training.

He told his father with great pride that he applied for and was accepted into paratrooper school. Milton signed up to spend another month in special training in hopes of making it in the airborne. The Sky Soldiers, as they called themselves, were one of the army's most elite units. They would jump out of planes usually ahead of advancing forces, or even behind enemy lines, to engage the enemy. They were prepared to be dropped into remote locations to take on the enemy on his home turf. Milton indeed wanted to prove himself. He was determined to make it not just in the army but as a member of one of its most heralded combat forces.

Milton's father acknowledged what his son told him and what he said that he wanted to achieve. He gave his blessing. More than that, he told his son to go for it, that he was proving himself, and that everyone in the family was proud of him.

Chapter III:
Sky Soldier

Milton took the early Saturday morning train back to the South and then on to Fort Benning. He was scheduled to report back to base Monday morning but wanted to make sure that he was there on time so he left Saturday and was back on base that Sunday, and ready to go. His cousin was not joining him on the return trip. Charles decided not to try for the airborne. Milton was on his own with total responsibility for his success or failure to demonstrate his worthiness to the folks back at home. Of equal if not more importance, he wanted to test and show himself that he was capable of becoming one of the best of the best fighting men.

Milton L Olive, III, was determined to make it in one of the army's toughest fighting groups: the 173rd Airborne Brigade, 503rd Infantry Regiment. He wanted to be a "Sky Soldier." This would not be an easy feat. The Sky Soldiers were a rough and tumble outfit, your quintessential rough-and-ready, bravest of the brave, as they often said of themselves. Milton knew very little of the history of the unit. Now he heard a bit more of it from Sergeant Wright, who had a longstanding nickname of "Get It Right" Wright. They heard from him and other NCOs who considered themselves "gatekeepers." What they meant by calling themselves that was that they were on a mission to make sure only the best made it as Sky Soldiers. They were determined to drum out the weaker elements and leave only the top echelon.

A basic requirement of the unit was to become familiar with its background.

"Is this a good idea?" Jamison asked the students. "Should you know the history of the organization you want to join?" It was rhetorical and he did not entertain any responses.

The 173rd began as an infantry unit in 1915 and saw its first action in World War I. It was later re-created as an airborne unit. The unit is seen as a "quick strike" force. A part of the 173rd Brigade was its 503rd Infantry Regiment with an illustrious history as a paratroop infantry group, formed in 1942 during the heart of World War II.

In short, Milton's designation as a member of Company B, Second Battalion, 503rd Infantry, 173rd Airborne Brigade, would mean that if he made the grade, he would be a member of an outfit that in all likelihood could be called upon to take first action in the defense of the United States of America or to deliver American might and military force anywhere in the world. As paratroopers, the unit was seen as one that could be delivered quickly to the site of battle. Whatever way the unit was deployed, it would likely be there in the forefront of the action.

Young Milton was not aware of the African-American historical component to what he was trying to achieve. He was joining a sizable number of African Americans who were part of the history of "Sky Soldiers." If he looked a little deeper into that history of the unit, and beyond what Sergeant Wright espoused, he would have found that long before he attempted to make it as a paratrooper, other African Americans led the way and opened doors for him, namely in the form of the 555th Paratroop Infantry of 1944 through 1947, a totally black outfit with black officers; a unit nicknamed the "Triple Nickels."

The twenty members of the 555th or Triple Nickels were the first black airborne soldiers.

They were also known as the "Colored Test Platoon" and the "Buffalo Nickels" (after the Buffalo Soldiers of the Indian Wars). They were the first African Americans trained at Fort Benning as Sky Soldiers. They were pioneers who blazed the trail that other black soldiers would later follow.

Although trained to see action abroad during World War II, they were deployed to the West Coast of the United States and spent most of their time fighting fires. There was a widespread belief among military intelligence that the Japanese were going to use incendiary balloons to cross the Pacific and then ignite the wooded areas on the West Coast. There were claims that this was in fact done. Others dispute those claims. At any rate, the Triple Nickels saw plenty of action as "Smoke Jumpers" which also became one of their nicknames. They helped to put out more than thirty major fires during the summer of 1945. Operating from Pendleton and Chico, California, the Triple Nickels responded to calls throughout the West, Northwest, and in states including Montana. After distinguished service to the nation, the 555th was disbanded in 1950.

Young Milton did not realize who broached the way for him to become a Sky Soldier. What he knew was that he was dedicated to becoming one. The question lingered in his mind: Could he make it? He was determined to do so though he heard the many stories about the rigor of the training.

The course was a little over three weeks. It was known to cause a sizable number of trainees to quit or be drummed out. Milton had never been one to shine physically in his youth. This was his second chance, as he saw it, his new opportunity to prove himself as a physical young man worthy of respect. He was mentally determined to survive the tests and demands ahead of him.

The United States Airborne School took charge of the training for all of those who wanted to become Sky Soldiers. Sergeant "Get It Right" Wright played the role of god and it was in his hands whether Milton would be judged worthy of membership into the elite corps.

The test for Milton began that Monday morning at 04 hundred hours with revelry and the coming together of the fifty-four volunteers comprising his class and wanting to make it into the airborne.

The course at Fort Benning was divided into three components: "Ground Week," "Tower Week," and "Jump Week." Through it all was a constant array of calisthenics and running to make sure that the trainees were in peak physical condition. The wake-up did not begin with chow, it began with push-ups: 50 of them to get the heart pumping fast, as Sergeant Wright liked to call it. They then began a series of jumping jacks, with hands overhead and legs extended, jumping with legs extended and then back to attention, repeating this with the yelling out of "one and two" "and one and two." They usually did between 50 to 100 jumping jacks.

Then came the running in place followed by "hitting the dirt" and "up and running." That particular exercise went on for a good ten minutes or more. Finally, mercifully, Wright yelled out: "At ease!" That did not mean slump over or lie on the ground and take it easy; it meant standing upright trying to catch one's breath while still showing signs of military discipline and decorum.

With the troopers "warmed up," the sergeant said it was time for "a nice walk-and-run in the park," as he jokingly termed it. In translation, it meant that Sergeant Wright was going to lead the men on a two-mile run; four miles when you count the return trip. It was also well known among men as the "puke walk." They called it that because so many of the troopers ended up vomiting along the way either there or on the return leg. There would be a lot of puking because Wright had them run every morning. Then there were the surprise days when the sergeant doubled the distance into four miles there and four miles back -- a puke-galore eight mile run. If the men slacked and did not go at the pace Wright was looking for, when they finished the last leg he put them through an intense round of additional calisthenics. The men named it "the sergeant's happy hour."

Throughout all the extensive calisthenics and daily runs, Milton held his own. Being slim may have worked in his favor during those long runs.

The heaviest of the soldiers found themselves at greatest risk of collapse or of puking because of exhaustion. Milton hung in there. He was not at the very front of the pack. He usually ran, admirably, somewhere in the upper half. Milton was a good trainee and making a daily statement that he had what it took to become a Sky Soldier.

After the "walk in the park" the troopers were allowed to take a quick shower and then move on to the mess hall for breakfast, which they were given forty minutes to complete. Milton felt that was a break since in basic training you usually were only allotted a chow-down time of thirty minutes or less. He welcomed the extra minutes to chew his food properly and to drink an abundance of liquids that all the troopers did after the "walk in the park."

When breakfast was completed, the men were soon reassembled for mid-day activities. The training focus was on the basic fundamentals of being a paratrooper. They were introduced to the device, with all the straps and harnesses and the internal chute, along with the reserve safety chute. Great detail and attention were taken to inform the men of the necessity of understanding every piece of equipment. Sergeant Wright and his team of instructors explained why the straps and harnesses were so crucial and had to be tight around the legs and shoulders.

The greatest amount of attention was paid to packing the chute and making sure that all lines were straight, neat and without any tangles. Failure to get it right, as the sergeant and others made the point time and again, could cause you your life. They heard Sergeant Wright say a million times, "Get it right! Get it right!" Thinking about it, jumping out of an airplane at a thousand or more feet, you wanted to make sure that you got it right and that everything worked correctly. There was basically no second chance except your backup chute. And if it was one of those jumps that was at the minimum safety height, one wondered if the backup was a realistic possibility, given how quick the ground was coming up to kiss you.

They talked about the art and philosophy of parachuting and a bit of the history of it. At times too, the sergeant and his team pointed with pride to the great history of the 173rd airborne and the 503rd. The point was made: that not all of them would be good enough to become Sky Soldiers, and those who did make it were the best of the best, and expected to be ready at a moment's notice to take on the enemy in any kind of situation.

"Would any of you be brave enough to jump out of a plane?" was Jamison's question to the students.

"With or without a parachute?" Someone in the back of the room replied without supplying a name. Laughs accompanied the remark.

"With one to make it easy," Jamison answered.

Several of the students said that they thought it could be fun. No one had actually parachuted and there was no real interest in the group to try it. Jamison was about to move on when Shanekwa asked him if he had ever skydived or would consider doing so?

"No," Jamison answered. "I have no intention in my life to jump out of a perfectly good airplane!"

There was a good amount of laughter before the story of Milton resumed.

Training at the base to become a Sky Soldier concentrated now on learning about the parachute and proper jumping techniques, along with the daily "walks in the park" and calisthenics that the sergeant always put them through. The basic fundamentals of the jump were gone over repeatedly until each man knew it by heart.

The men were divided up into teams and packed and repacked parachutes for hour after hour over several days. Each man in the team was required to learn every part of the chute and to identify it when questioned by one of the instructors. The instructor team watched every group intensely commenting on the need to keep lines straight and taut and to fold correctly with the proper distance and seams. To make a mistake, they reminded you, would cost you your life. This went on for a very intensive week, practicing every day except Sunday for at least six hours off and on in total each day.

Some of the men dropped out that first week. It was most likely the long "walks in the park" that were as much to blame as the long hours spent packing, unpacking, and repacking parachutes. There were those who simply were not physically fit enough to be Sky Soldiers, despite having made it through basic training, and they were eliminated from the group. Milton hung in there and finished his first week with flying colors.

After all of the talk, discussion, and packing and repacking, they began practicing off of jump stands, how to land appropriately; how to tuck and roll when you hit the ground. The drills were repeated countless times. They discussed the mechanics of the chute, how the pulling of the directional cords worked, how to correct your drift, and more demonstrations about the proper way to hit the ground with the least amount of force, to roll with the impact and to quickly recover and gain control of your chute once you are on the ground. Finally, the instructors deemed the trainees ready to take it to the next level which was the jump tower.

It was known as "Tower Week." The men were being prepared to take their first practice jumps from the towers. There were three jump towers at Fort Benning. Originally, when the fort was designed and first built, there were four jump towers. A tornado destroyed one of them in 1954. For whatever reason, the military decided not to rebuild the fourth tower and reinforced the remaining three.

The three would prove to be more than enough in training the constant flow of military men who were coming through the program to be initiated into the fraternity of Sky Soldiers. The towers were 250 feet each. The trooper would be strapped into an open chute which then ascended to the top of the tower via mechanical pulleys. Once at the top, the chute was fully opened and released with the individual jumper allowed to float freely from the tower, having to adjust and control his dissent on the way down. Typically, one man at a time went up and then was released.

Sergeant Wright or another one of his instructor, via a powerful megaphone, barked out instructions to the dissenting trooper, telling him to either pull right or pull left to adjust his dissent, and try to land in a certain area. The trooper would constantly be reminded on the way down to tuck and roll when he hit the ground. Some of the jumpers actually landed on their feet with no need to tuck and roll, which was a perfect jump and one you could typically not count on.

However you landed you had to next grab and pull in the chute, control it and bring it to a stop.

There were discussions about "what if." Those "what ifs" included, if you happened to land in a tree, how to descend from it. They discussed water landings and how to quickly free yourself from the chute or risk being pulled underwater. They talked about how once you did land the necessity to bury or otherwise hide your parachute, keeping in mind that time was always of the essence.

Milton was downright frightened when the day came for his first jump from the tower. His heart was in his throat just like that of everyone else who ascended the 250 foot tower for the first time, realizing that once you reached the top, the chute would be released and you would descend to the earth solely with the support of the parachute. He was also mindful that the practice jump was not without its risks. It was the exceptional year when no one was injured. There had been some serious injuries and several deaths in recent years. It was the military and preparation for combat was itself risky and potentially deadly business.

When it was Milton's turn at the tower he did not hesitate. He remembered his training and meticulous preparation. Hooked up with the harness to the chute, he could hear the crane as it began lifting him up to the top of the tower. Once there, after a few seconds, he heard Sergeant Wright give the command: "Let deploy." The chute was released.

There was a short free fall as the chute opened fully. Milton recalled that part of the way down was nice, almost fun, relaxing, as he floated in the air. All too quickly, the ground was upon him and he could hear the instructor saying pull left you are floating too far right. He followed the commands keeping his chute lines straight. Finally, as they warned him the ground was there and he prepared to tuck and roll. He did not have to tuck and roll. Milton landed on his feet and was able to run the short distance pulling the parachute down, gaining control and quickly wrapping it up as he was trained. His was an exemplary tower jump.

The youngster from Chicago was well on his way to becoming a Sky Soldier. There were those who failed the tower jump. And there were those who when looking at the apparatus and realizing for the first time that they would be lifted some 250 feet in the air and then literally let loose to float down by nothing more than the parachute – decided that being a Sky Soldier was not for them. Milton L. Olive, III, was not one of them.

During the "Tower Week" Milton made a jump each day. So by the time of the sixth day, he felt that he really had the hang of it and was relatively relaxed and in control of his chute all the way up and all the way down. He never made another jump in which he landed perfectly on his feet. They were excellent jumps nevertheless. Tuck and roll came in handy and he performed the maneuver quite well. He heard the sergeant say more than once to him those magic words: "Good jump private" – high praise indeed from "Get It Right" Wright. Milton's last jump from the tower was that Saturday and he performed it without a hitch.

The third week of training was the real deal: "Jump Week." It meant exactly what it said. This was the week that you would go up in an airplane and at between 1000 and 1200 feet, make your first real parachute jump. The first day of that week was spent taking great care and going over the packing and repacking of the parachute, and talking about the actual job that was going to come first thing on Tuesday morning. Sergeant Wright even dispensed with his usual "walk in the park." After all, by now they were either in shape or would never get there. Moreover, he did not want the men to be fatigued when taking their first jump.

It was barely daylight when they boarded the aircraft for the first actual jump. Sergeant Wright advised the men against having breakfast that morning, because it was uncertain how some might react to that first time jumping out of a plane. As he put it to the troopers, "There is nothing worse than jumping through a spray of vomit." Those remarks gained some laughter but for some others it was simply a note of terror because this was, after all, their very first jump from an airplane with the real possibility of something going wrong and nothing between you and the ground except your backup safety chute, if you did not panic and had time enough to deploy it, after cutting away your main chute. These were all points that went through the mind of each man on the plane.

They were all seated as the aircraft took off. They knew who would be first at the door. They knew to hook up, and they knew to move when you were tapped by the sergeant followed with the command to "Jump!" Actually, it was a bit more than a tap that the sergeant and his assistant gave to each man. It was almost a push. Indeed, if you hesitated at the door you would have been pushed out. More than one trooper hesitated a second or two, requiring an actual shove out the door.

The flight took no time to reach the 1200 feet for the jumps. Sergeant Wright yelled out to everyone that it was jump time; it was green light. He told them all to stand and get ready. They moved over to the port side. The sergeant then gave then the order to "hook up," which they did to the wire cord above them leading to the open door. The first soldier in line was instructed to take his mark at the door with each soldier no more than arm's length behind the other. With Wright looking out and his assistant near, the green jump light came on, which meant that the pilot was telling them they were at the jump site and at the appropriate altitude. It was time to jump. Next came the magic words from the sergeant: "Jump, jump, jump!" Each time he commanded "jump," another Sky Soldier went through the door and out into the swirly bond, a freefall and the terror and the exhilaration that came with stepping out of an aircraft with nothing between mother earth and you but the silk of your parachute.

Milton was number four in line. He could hear the command "jump." He heard it repeated until it was his turn. Before he could give it more thought he was at the door, heard the word "jump," and received the firm pat on his back. He went through the door and into the sky. As he fell his heart was again in his throat until he heard that thankful pop and felt the jerk of the rip cord opening his chute. His descent slowed in midair. He knew that all was likely to be well and that his chute was open and doing its thing. His training took hold and he steered clear of all possible trees as he floated to earth.

As the ground rose to meet him, upon contact he tucked and rolled and immediately came to his feet and started wrestling his chute in. The jump site that they chose was one that had very few trees. They did not want to test their new troopers to the full limits of survival by putting them in extreme danger, although they talked constantly about how to circumvent trees, and if lodged in one how to extricate yourself properly. The greatest danger of landing in a tree was that you might break your neck or sustain other serious injuries due to the branches. Troopers too often forfeited their lives owing to landing in trees during a combat mission.

Milton was amazed at how quickly the jump came to an end. No sooner did he step out of that door that he began to see and finally touch earth. He made an excellent landing although he was not able to land on his feet and remain standing. It was fairly windy. Indeed, the jump would have been called off if the wind was more than twenty miles per hour. That was routine to call off the jump if the wind velocity was that high or higher. In reality, troopers might be expected to jump in much higher velocity. There was no need for the extra endangerment in training, or so was the philosophy of the commander of the jump school. After all, as some of them liked to say, "You didn't need to practice actual jumps too much. It only took one bad jump to kill you."

The troopers upon landing all gathered together, reflecting and chatting away about the experience, many with smiles and giggling. Sergeant Wright understood all of this and allowed for the merriment and exchange of reflections to continue for a good half an hour. He knew what it was like when you took your first jump and the delight of having come through safely. When he did call the men to attention, he reminded them that every Sky Soldier vividly recalled his first jump. That statement conveyed something to the men that did not go unnoticed. Wright called them "Sky Soldiers." It was the first time they heard a definitive indication that they were meeting the standards and on their way to their goal.

The sergeant directed the men aboard the waiting buses that took them back to camp where their first assignment, with chutes carried by each man, was to divide up into teams of four to repack each chute within that team. The thinking was developed over the years since the very start of the 173rd Airborne to have groups work on the chutes. That way, if one man missed something, it was a much greater likelihood that one of the others three would catch it and correct it. It also helped to build the bonds between the men in that each one concentrated hard on doing a perfect job because, after all of that, the repacked chutes were randomly distributed. It meant that you were likely not to get the chute that you personally repacked. You counted upon each other and your group to pack the parachutes right. You depended upon each other for your well-being and your life. It was exactly what the military wanted. It was a golden rule that the 173rd Airborne practiced and lived or died by.

There was more than enough time left in the day for a second jump. There would be no second jump that day and most days. You took only one jump each day. Again, the thinking was that you probably needed only a few jumps to get the hang of it. Taking more than that was too risky and not enough accomplished in terms of learning. If you did not get it the first time, you certainly got it on the second try. There would be a jump each remaining day.

Milton's next jumps were all exhilarating experiences for him. By his fourth jump, he actually looked down upon exiting the aircraft, which was something you were trained to avoid because of the possible fear factor. He so overcame his fear that he wanted to get a glimpse of how high up in the air he was upon descending the plane. He did so, telling himself as he left the plane the words that would stay with him forever each time he jumped: "Oh God I am yours."

Jump Week was almost at an end. There was only one more jump remaining: it was the dreaded night jump. All troopers trained at parachute school did the familiar or infamous night jump. It was the ultimate test of nerves and strict adherence to order. It was one thing to descend out of a plane in daylight. It was something else to step through a door 1000 or more feet up in the air, and not seeing or sensing anything below except darkness. The only reference point you might possibly glimpse was a light coming from the far-off barracks. If you were following the jump rules of not looking down, you did not see those lights; you merely stepped through a door into complete and utter darkness with nothing but you and your parachute.

A thousand different things went through Milton's mind as it did for all the other jumpers no doubt, including the big one: "What if something goes wrong? What if I really do have to use my emergency chute? Would I be able to see the line to cut the main chute away?" Milton found himself positioning the knife that he and all the paratroopers carried with them in case of an emergency. He was likely not the only trooper who placed his knife at the ready for the night jump.

It was a Saturday when they took the night jump. The carrier plane purposefully took off after 22 hundred hours. The jump school through its years of training paratroopers came to the conclusion that the later the actual night jump, the better. Two factors were at work here: first, it was certainly dark enough at 22 hundred to make sure there was very little if any ambient light that would make it easier on the jumpers; and second, lights out in the barracks was at 21 hundred hours. Going at 22 hundred also meant that some of the troopers no doubt were sleepy and had that additional burden to contend with during the jump. All of these factors, the paratrooper school concluded, were good for the trainees to get them ready for the possibility, which was a real one, of having to make night parachute jumps if called upon to do so and under the stress of combat.

The plane loaded up that night and rumbled down the runway and lifted off. It quickly reached the 1200 feet altitude and Sergeant Wright gave them the command to rise and hook up. Milton was number two in line this time. They had boarded according to height, with the shortest men at the rear, which placed them first in jump order. The sergeant noted that it was green light and the troopers all rose and hooked up with the first jumper at the door gripping the sides. Then Wright gave the order, "Jump," accompanied by the friendly yet firm pat on the back.

Before Milton could give it much thought it was his turn and with the command "jump," he "hit the silk" and was on his way down in pitch darkness. He relished how quiet it was and how serene for about a split second until he heard that familiar and comforting sound indicating that his parachute deployed. No need for the knife that was in close reach. He looked up and saw the light of the moon and knew he was making a nice and comfortable glide to earth. As he looked down, he could not see anything and this gave him a momentary sense of fright. It was completely black. He imagined in that split second that perhaps he was going to land in a tree or water. In either case he better be ready and he was concentrating on what would be his next move in either encounter. Before he could give it too much thought the earth was upon him and in the last second he saw that he was not fixing to hit anything except the ground. He bent his knees and prepared for impact; tucked and rolled. He was down successfully and quickly reeled in his parachute.

Milton passed the ultimate jump. He mastered the course and could hear other troopers in the night congratulating themselves and each other. He joined in. Several troopers, not more than twenty feet away from him, were yelling "We made it!" Huddling together they complimented each other on the successful night jump and the conclusion to jump school. Moreover, there had not been one casualty during the training.

After allowing the men to chat and exchange congratulations on the successful night jump, Sergeant Wright, who often jumped last after the men, did so that night. He wanted to be with them in both the experience and the final congratulations. With his chute in hand, the sergeant walked over to the men and said in the loudest and clearest voice, "You've done it. "Congratulations, Sky Soldiers!"

Several of the men could not help themselves and blurted in reply to the sergeant, "Thank you Sergeant 'Get It Right' Wright!"

Sergeant Wright smiled the biggest smile. He knew that over the years the trainees gave him the nickname "Get It Right." He considered the nickname a badge of honor, and he loved it.

Milton made it as a Sky Soldier. He and his fellow troopers were now bona fide members of the U. S. Army Airborne. Milton wrote to his parents back in Chicago, telling them with the greatest pride, "I am now a Sky Soldier." He wrote to cousin Barbara telling her that he was a paratrooper and already made several jumps, including a night one. She was cautious and reflective in her reply.

Learning to parachute was one thing. But what next? There was much talk around Fort Benning that the training the men received was more likely to be put into practice right away than at any time since the Korean War. There was talk galore about the growing conflict in Vietnam.

"How great!" Yousef blurted out. "So the young brother is a Sky Soldier, ready to fight, kill and – for this place. So what? Does it make sense for him to be a Sky Soldier? He's a black man in a country than didn't give two cents about him and he's fixing to lay his life on the line if need be for whatever the powers that be tell him that they want him to do. That doesn't make sense to me. Mister Jamison."

"So, Yousef, you obviously think that Milton has made a terrible mistake, a point you have made now several times," Jamison recapped.

"Dog gone right!" Yousef did not hold back. "Why would you go and fight for this place? It simply doesn't make any sense for me. If I'm treated equally, I have equality, I'm seen as good as anybody else, and I will not have to put up with this race and color crap every day, then I'm willing to say yeah, I have an equal share in America and I should fight for it. Since that is not the case, no, I don't see why I should be joining up in the white man's army to go off and do his fighting."

"Well," Jamison asserted. "Yousef has made his point again. Do the rest of you agree or disagree with him? What do you think?"

Jamison could see that Shanekwa wanted to say something so he called on her. "Shanekwa, I can see that you are bursting with some ideas. Please go ahead."

"Well, Mister J, it's a tough question. Yousef, who I usually disagree with it, may have a point here."

She could hear Yousef in the background murmuring some remarks that sounded like it's about time she started to understand the brother.

"Mister J, when Yousef said this is not his country I think I understand what he means," Shanekwa continued. "And Milton was back in the 1960s and things were far worse for people of color back then than they are here in the 21st century. I don't know whether he was right or wrong in joining the military and wanting to be a paratrooper. At the same time, we all have the right to be what we want to be. Right? I mean, if he sees his future in the military, I think he has a right to go for it. I can't tell other people what to do. We can look back from the present and say maybe that war was wrong or maybe he made a wrong decision. Keep in mind that it was his life and his decision to make. Right?"

Jamison looked around the room to ask if there were other students who wanted to share their thoughts about Milton's decision. He could see the contemplative look on the students' faces. They were clearly wrestling with the issues of whether or not you should fight for a country that does not treat you as an equal. Jamison saw a good opportunity to raise some other issues and questions thanks to Yousef's very blunt criticism of Milton's decision.

"Let me ask you all this," Jamison posited. "What do you think of the argument that some have made, in fact many have made throughout the history of this nation that black folk should fight and be a part of America's war effort if they hoped to ever be equal citizens. What do you think of that argument? Can you expect the nation to treat you as an equal if you don't take on equal responsibilities?"

Yousef could not resist. Before anyone raised a hand he simply blurted out: "I've said it before and I'll say it again: Why should you have to prove that you are equal to be treated equal? We are citizens of the United States of America. Right? I heard that you, Mister Jamison, are always talking about the Constitution, the Bill of Rights, and all of that other good stuff in your classes. We've heard stuff about the founding fathers and some of that. And I know that I am going to hear much more of it when I have to take American history in order to graduate. But aren't we equals according to the Constitution and all those other fancy documents that were put in place to say and spell out what a citizen is? If that's the case, then why do we have to prove that we are equals? We shouldn't have to."

"Is Yousef right?" Jamison asked the others. "Do you have to prove yourself as a citizen or by virtue of the Constitution are you simply entitled to all the rights and privileges of a citizen? Are there duties to the nation that you must perform?"

Even Shanekwa was moving ever closer to Yousef's repeated position: "I think Yousef is right, although I hate to agree with him. You shouldn't have to prove your right to equality if you are entitled to be treated equal. We know for a fact that black folks have not been treated as equals in the society and are not treated equally despite there being a black man now in the White House. I think we all know that racism is still well and alive in the good old USA. We shouldn't have to prove that we are equals to get what is due us."

There was a short burst of applause from some of the students in support of the oration. Jamison stood back and enjoyed the exchange between the students. He let it go on and on. He saw no need to intervene as students were wrestling with the issues and both sides were making strong points. He heard several take the position that if you wanted equality you had to fight for it, and that no one gives it to you. At the same time, he heard others say that unless they are treated equally they see no need of serving this nation. They were, on their own, raising questions about fairness, equality, and what citizenship actually means.

Jamison was now smiling away as his captive group bought into the intellectual, political, and social importance of the story of Milton Olive and what his decisions and his life might teach us all.

"Mister J, I see you there smiling. Do you like this?" Shanekwa asked.

"You bet I do," Jamison replied. With all the students looking intently at him, he said to them all: "I couldn't be happier with the discussion we're engaged in. You are wrestling with important issues about citizenship, freedom, equality, personal choice, values, and all that other good stuff that is a part of the adult world. You have to make decisions as an adult. You also have to make them as a young person, right. All of you have to make decisions – – right now. You have to make decisions about how you will act. You have to make decisions about choosing to act up or not to, to be civil or not to, to fight in the hallways or not to!"

Mr. Jamison had driven home again the initial point behind him pulling them into his classroom. "We can learn a lot from Milton L Olive and his life and the sacrifice he made," Jamison reiterated.

"Go on Mister J, are you going to finish telling us about what happened to Milton?" Shanekwa asked.

"Well, Shanekwa, you know what happened to him in the end. You have heard the story before. I am glad to go ahead and finish telling the story if you students are truly interesting in hearing about the rest of Milton's life?"

One of the most unlikely voices in the room chimed in to say: "I want to hear what happened to the brother. I can guess how it ends, but I would like to know, I want to hear the details of this so I can learn from it, really," declared Yousef.

His remarks confirmed that Milton Olive's story was a gripping one from which the young people were learning. They were digesting the point that life was all about decisions and choices and the key was to make the right ones.

"Milton made his decision and made the grade. He was officially a Sky Soldier," Jamison reminded everyone. "The next thing would be deployment. Do you know what deployment means?"

Most of the students nodded in the affirmative that they understood what it meant and indeed one blurted it out: "It means being called up! It means being sent into action!" Murphy said. "It means the same thing as happened to my brother. He went in the military thinking that he was going to get an education and learn a technical skill that would help him get a good job when he was discharged. He though there would be a lot of fun stuff. He didn't think much about being in the military might mean that you have to fight if the country goes to war. That's exactly what happened to him; sort of like what I guess happened to Milton. My brother is over in Afghanistan right now after, as I told you earlier, serving in Iraq. Hopefully he will live through it and make it home safe. At any rate, he's doing his duty. And I do think that's the role of the citizen. You do your duty. You can always think everything will be the way you like it in this country or any other. You try to make it better. You don't just refuse to serve because everything is not perfect; at least that's my opinion."

"Thank you Murphy," Jamison said.

With jump school completed, Milton and the other new Sky Soldiers were given a two-week furlough. It was time for him to head home to Chicago before reporting back for deployment.

Milton Olive in uniform at home

Olive in Nam

Milton Olive senior and wife Antoinette accepting their son's Medal of Honor
from President Johnson
(Standing directly behind the Olives and President are Mayor Richard J. Daley,
Lt. Jimmy Stanford and PFC. John Foster)

Olive-Harvey Community College in Chicago, named after two hometown heroes
of the Vietnam War: Medal of Honor Recipients Milton L. Olive, III, and
Carmel Benton Harvey, Jr.

Olive Park by Lake Michigan in downtown Chicago

Chapter IV:
Deployment

Back home in Chicago, Milton hit all of his usual spots: Maxwell Street, Jim's, the park along Lake Michigan near downtown, and an occasional movie -- at all times fully dressed in his uniform. The two-week furlough came and went with the blink of an eye.

He was wide awake when the train arrived back at Fort Benning. Most of the men were arriving back on base that weekend in preparation for roll call bright and early Monday morning. They knew too that this would be the day, or at least sometime midweek, that they would hear where they were being assigned.

Graduation was over. Milton was a full-fledged and ready-to-go Sky Soldier. It was only a question of where he would be deployed. Everyone knew or at least they thought they did. The Sky Soldiers and the Marines were traditionally among the first to fight. With that in mind, it seemed most likely that they would be deployed to Southeast Asia, to the emerging new war in Vietnam.

When Milton joined the army, he knew very little if anything about what was happening in Vietnam. U.S. forces were ramping up ever since August 1964. In particular, that was the month of the Tonkin Gulf incident. The alleged firing of the North Vietnamese Navy on the USS Maddox was cited as justification for a declaration of war against the North Vietnamese. Indeed, President Lyndon Johnson called for sweeping executive powers to be able to use military force to protect the allies in South Vietnam and, of course, to assert America's right to defend itself against any unwarranted attack. Later investigations concluded that the USS Maddox was not fired upon. This was a moot point at the moment.

President Johnson received the authorization he wanted from the U.S. Congress to use military force where the president deemed necessary. The arguments were persuasive to Congress which passed the Tonkin Gulf Resolution on August 7, 1964 by a vote of 88 to 2 in the Senate and 416 to 0 in the House. The War in Vietnam was up and running.

Johnson almost immediately began increasing troop numbers in Vietnam. One of the first units called to deployment was Milton's unit, the 173rd Airborne Brigade. It was on a Monday at Fort Benning, at 07:30 hours – a late or relatively late

start in the morning by Fort Benning standards –
that Milton's entire company was called to order.

The sun was already up and gave extra warmth
to the bright day and an extra boost although the
men did not need it. They were fired up to hear
their orders, with Sergeant Wright and other
sergeants calling all of the units to attention. The
sergeants reported "all present and accounted for"
to their respective officers who verbally passed
confirmation up the ladder until it was reported to
the Base Commander who took the microphone
to address all the Sky Soldiers.

The Base Commander, Colonel Lamar Welch,
a WWII veteran, a master parachutist, and longtime Sky Soldier, gave the men a short yet
emphatic message:

"You men, you Sky Soldiers, are fully trained,
ready to eat fire, and able to stump any enemy of
the United States into dust. You are the finest of

the finest and hence you will be immediately sent to that part of the world where you are needed most, to defend this nation against the threat of communism and to help our allies in Southeast Asia. God bless you."

This was the first time that officially Milton had heard the term Southeast Asia, and he and the others heard it directly from Colonel Welch himself. Milton knew enough to know that it meant that he and the rest of the Sky Soldiers, and probably all the troops there at Fort Benning, were on their way to Vietnam. He was getting a quick education about that part of the world, although he still knew very little about what was actually going on. What he heard around the barracks and on military news was that communism must be contained and that U. S. allies in that region needed American support to keep their country strong, independent, and free.

At least that was what he and the other soldiers heard.

The guessing game was over. Not only that, Colonel Welch informed them that they would all be shipping out in less than 24 hours. He then dismissed them so that they might enjoy an unusually long and leisurely breakfast, with the final words: "You men have a full hour to eat this morning. I want you to relax and have a good meal. We need you strong, we want you confident, and we want you ready at 05 hundred tomorrow morning in full gear, ready to ship out. So enjoy your breakfast, you deserve the very best. And by the way, this morning we are having steak and eggs; just the very thing that fighting men need before they go out and kick butt!"

The men responded with yells and applause!

After the company was dismissed, many mingled about chatting about being sent to

Vietnam. Others made a quick beeline for the mess hall to chow down on that endless supply of steak and eggs. Yet others, like Milton, sought solitude to think about what was ahead. Milton returned to the barracks, thinking hard as he started packing his belongings. He was more interested in being ready to go early that next morning than he was to get a belly full of steak and eggs. He was dedicated to the cause, a Sky Soldier in the fullest sense of the term.

"Did he think for a moment about where he was going or what he was about to do, what he was being order to do?" Yousef asked. "This brother is fixing to be sent on to fight against other brown brothers way across the world. The same brown brothers who have done nothing to him."

"What do others think?" Jamison inquired.

"I would have been scared to death to have to go," Shanekwa responded.

"It's Miller time!" Murphy spouted. "It comes a time when you have to stand up and be counted and be a man! Milton was no different than my brother. The time comes when you have to ante up, and that is what he was being urged to do and he stepped forward to do it. Yousef can say whatever he wants. This is my country. It's Yousef's too whether he believes it or not, and we have to fight for it."

"Spoken like a true white man," Yousef retorted. "Why don't you white folks just go over and cleanup your own mess rather than having black folks involved in it. We don't own a thing in this country and we're supposed to go and kill or be killed. That's what I find so crazy about all of this. In my opinion, Milton was a very misguided young brother."

"I think we know your position on this by now Yousef. What do others have to say?" Jamison posited. "Was Milton just a confused young brother? Or was he someone who saw very clearly his responsibility and his mission? What do others think?"

"Yousef just keeps saying the same stuff over and over," Murphy chided. "Say something new."

"I will say something new when you say something new," Yousef fired back.

"Hold it right there. Let's remain civil to one another. We can agree to disagree like rational thinking adults. Be courteous even if you strongly disagree with one another," Jamison reminded thee two.

"Why do we have to fight?" A new voice joined in from one of the girls sitting near the very back of the room, and who had not spoken a single word through all of the previous exchanges.

"And your name?" Jamison asked.

"My name is Barbara."

"Well, Barbara, tell us more."

Barbara continued: "I mean, why do we have to fight anyway? People talk all the time about being civilized and having good sense and how wrong it is to be violent, how wrong it is to hurt someone, how wrong it is certainly to shoot someone. We shoot each other all the time anyway around here and all around where I live. I hear from my mother and I hear from the preacher all the time that 'thou shall not kill.' Well, if that's the case, why do we say it's ok for Milton to go somewhere and kill or be killed? It simply doesn't make sense to me; grown folks, shooting and killing one another over what? I don't know a lot about the Vietnam thing except what I've seen on TV and in the movies. That place is a long way away to go to fight. Vietnam is certainly not in America. It's not down the street from us or a nearby state or country. Folk should have been meeting to discuss things and talk and to make peace or at least to find a way to work out their differences. That's what I think." Barber finished and then leaned back in her seat.

Jamison did not have to say anything after that. There was a free flow of ideas among the students. They went back and forth to each other questioning the necessity of war, the rightness of war, the madness of war, and whether it makes sense for anybody to kill or be killed. It was exactly the kind of discussion of which any teacher would have been proud. The students were debating the philosophical, ethical, moral or immoral nature of war. After a good ten minutes of spirited yet civil exchange of ideas, Jamison resumed the account of Milton's deployment.

Milton did not make it to the mess hall to enjoy the sumptuous breakfast that morning. Finished packing, he lay across his bonk with arms folded behind his head and staring up at the barrack's ceiling. He thought about what was happening and entertained the realization that he was likely going into combat, going into harm's way. Thus far, everything had been predictable in a sense. It was training. It was at times stressful and other times dangerous. It, however, was not the real war, the one that he was about to step foot in. Milton questioned himself too about whether he would be able to kill someone if required. He considered it not an easy matter or an easy question. Of course he was right. He imagined himself out there on patrol with his loaded M-14 with orders to kill or be killed. Again the question: Could he do it? He wondered if he might freeze in the face of the enemy. It was no longer a practice drill. It would be men that he shot at, and they would shoot back.

His thoughts made perfect sense. Milton was following the tradition and mindset of countless other men who went into battle for the first time. Anyone, facing the grave danger that lay ahead, second guessed themselves. Would he be able to do his job or would he turn tail and run? These were tough questions he asked of himself. He was also using this opportunity to reinforce his determination to do his job, to do his duty as he saw it, and to make the folks back home proud. Even more, he wanted to make his fellow soldiers proud of him. He had bonded with them. They were a band of brothers. They were all Sky Soldiers whose motto was to always be brave and true. Milton was psyching himself up for the challenge to come.

Before this moment, he had not thought much about Vietnam. As a matter of fact, as he reminded himself, he knew very little about the history or the place. He was not a student of geopolitics, Vietnamese nationalism, French colonialism, or the new American interest and role in that part of the world. In point of fact, if given a world map, Milton would not have been able to easily pinpoint Southeast Asia and Vietnam. Nevertheless, he was on his way there.

He continued laying back, looking up at the ceiling and contemplating what tomorrow and the days after that might bring. What he did know was that he was determined to prove himself worthy of the military and worthy of the patch that he proudly wore on his shoulder. It was the insignia of the Sky Soldiers, the airborne of which he was a newly minted member.

Milton believed in America and its leadership. It was clear to him that President Johnson wanted the nation to win this new war and that it was a war that would likely be over quickly. At least that was what most people were saying. Milton was anxious to do his part.

He prepared for the long flight to Vietnam. Milton heard that the travel would take several days for them to arrive there. He thought about how hot it might be and what "the jungle" would be like. Whether what he heard was true or not he did not know.

Although Milton missed breakfast, he did make it over to the mess hall for lunch. The steak and eggs were long since gone. The soup was good and hot, the beef burgers delicious, and the plate of vegetables quite tasty. The conversation during lunch was also good although Milton never made close friends though most of the men were not much older than him. One forgets that those who typically fight America's wars are usually from 18 to 22 years of age. They are our young men who have either voluntarily, or otherwise, stepped forward to go into harm's way.

You knew that the company was getting ready for deployment because there were no further demands made on the time of the troopers that day. No one had them do exercises or anything else that might be considered work or interference with their thoughts about being shipped out. Milton's voyage would happen tomorrow. For now, the base was in a relaxed mood. The entire place seemed to be in tribute to those who were about to go forth and fight, and risk making the supreme sacrifice – if necessary – of their life.

After lunch Milton strolled about the base looking at the jump towers and remembering that sense of fright and his first jump from the 250 foot tower. He also recalled the exhilaration he felt floating to earth and knowing that he succeeded in that mission. He was a proud young man. He walked, he contemplated, and he looked for solace within himself. He was no different than some of the athletes he knew about, or at least he thought. They too, he reasoned, must have thought about the big game and psyched themselves up for their performance. They may have questioned whether they would be good enough that day or make mistakes. They too must have questioned their own ability with a certain amount of doubt. It was not that Milton was scared. He was exhilarated and at the same time felt an incredible burden of responsibility. Yes, he was questioning whether he would perform well under fire or succumb to the human frailty of self-preservation when faced with ultimate danger. He told himself over and again "I will do my job. I will do my job."

The base was showing a movie that evening that he gladly partook of as did most of the Sky Soldiers. They had two showing of the movie to accommodate all of those who wanted to see it. One showing was right after dinner at 19 hundred hours and another one began right after that at 20 hundred hours. It was a shortened version of the film, "To Hell and Back," starring Audie Murphy.

Milton watched the film with intense interest. At the beginning of the film, a commanding officer spoke on camera about the heroics of Audie Murphy during World War II, mentioning that the young man from Texas had earned virtually every medal the army offered. Milton thought about how great were Murphy's accomplishments. He heard of Murphy's background as a poor youngster from a farm community and his struggle to achieve something in life. Murphy was small like Milton. Both of them were only 5 feet and a few inches tall, and both were little in terms of body weight. Milton noted the similarities with much interest. With the exception of skin color, he thought of himself as much like Audie Murphy, a youngster who did not have a great amount of expectations that he would amount to much, and one who was dedicated to being the very best he could be and to serve with bravery in face of the enemy.

Milton and the other soldiers watched "To Hell and Back" as not only a movie but perhaps a statement of individual merit and what they themselves might hope to achieve or at least the superior level at which they hoped to perform when faced with the kinds of obstacles that

Murphy overcame. This was, no doubt, exactly what the army hoped would be the impact of the viewing.

Milton envisioned himself in similar situations as Murphy and vowed to rise to the occasion and be brave. He choked with emotion when he saw Murphy at the end of the film standing on the parade ground and receiving the nation's highest military commendation, the Medal of Honor. He could not help but notice that Murphy at the time was not much older than himself; only a bit past his 19th birthday. Milton too felt that he could perform as well. He knew he wanted to be among the brave and those with medals and other accolades. He wanted his folks back in Chicago and Lexington and everyone who knew him to be proud of him. This would be his opportunity, he thought; if not to win a medal, at least to do his job well at a level that he distinguished himself as being a top-flight soldier. This meant a great deal to him.

For security reasons, none of the men at the base were allowed to make phone calls home and to alert their loved ones that they were shipping out. In fact, they were told in no uncertain terms not to mention to anyone any details of their deployment. Milton readily followed that order as did the rest of his comrades. After walking a bit more, and chatting on occasion with other troopers here and there, he was finally ready to hit the sack. Indeed, he was eager to get to sleep because he knew that meant that it would only be a short period of time before he was woke and on his way to becoming a real combat soldier.

He did not easily fall asleep that night. His mind kept wandering: What would Vietnam be like? Would it be hot and humid over there? How tough will the enemy be? What did it feel like to be in a live combat situation with bullets flying and bombs bursting in air? Yes, he harbored a number of thoughts that kept him from falling asleep. There were others on the base with similar insomnia to be sure.

Milton's mind worked nonstop that night, so much so that he did not remember falling asleep until he heard revelry the next morning. It was time to get up, get dressed, chow down, and report to the rally point at the base air strip, as ordered and in full combat gear including his weapon. He and the rest of his fellow troopers were to board the huge cargo planes that would ferret them the long journey to Southeast Asia.

There was a feeling of exhilaration and excitement on the part of Milton and certainly among the other soldiers. This was what they had trained for and now was upon them. After some hardy very early morning chow, Milton and his brother Sky Soldiers were in formation and ready to travel to the other side of the world.

Chapter V:

The Nam

It looked like everyone at the entire fort was out on the field that morning. Milton realized for the first time that he never actually knew how many men were at Fort Benning. He looked around before they were called to attention and could see thousands of men. Ten thousand was his best guess, not all of whom were going to make the journey. The sergeants were reporting to the lieutenants and the lieutenants to the captains and then finally to Colonel Welch who gave the men greetings that morning and told them that they were shipping out and going to do God's work. He wished them the best of luck and Godspeed to their destination. With those few words each battalion was ordered out one by one to the airfield where they would board planes to take them to Southeast Asia.

The planes that awaited Milton and his fellow troopers were the biggest aircraft he had ever seen in his life. Though the planes that they took the practice jumps from were big enough, they did not compare to these monstrously large birds. Milton was certainly no expert on the subject of aircraft since the first plane ride for him was on the one that he jumped from during parachute training. What he saw in front of him should have been impressive since they were, indeed, the biggest transport planes in the military, the new

C-141 Starlifters, capable of carrying troops, vehicles, armaments and anything else.

The men counted out from one to one hundred and then were told to start boarding the planes, with one hundred soldiers assigned to each aircraft. Milton was amazed at the amount of room on the plane as he took his seat and strapped himself in. This was also his first time on a jet. The aircraft at the base were propeller driven. The C-141 Starlifter was not only much bigger, and with extraordinary carrying capacity, it was also much faster given its jet propulsion.

The pilots throttled up and the big bird rumbled down the runway and in seconds Milton and his comrades were airborne. He was wide awake during the takeoff and for the next hour or two. Then, however, he found himself extremely relaxed and eerily comfortable. Shortly after that, Milton was fast asleep and oblivious to the first leg of the travel. He did awake when the plane landed in California, or that at least was the rumored landing site according to some of the men on board. The plane took on additional fuel but the men were not allowed to deplane to stretch their legs. They were allowed to stretch and move about on the plane until fueling was completed. Then back into their seats for the next phase of the journey.

Milton stayed awake for much of the second phase of the journey even though there was nothing to view except sky and clouds and occasionally to get a peek of the ocean way beneath them. He was never sure where they landed next. Some on board said it was Hawaii while others said it was someplace near South Korea. Whatever the truth might have been, they were almost at their destination.

After a total of more than thirty hours of flying, the plane finally landed. Milton was wide awake and could see out of one of the few windows on the plane. Where they were looked very lush, very tropical, and very unfamiliar to the Chicago boy.

After the big bird taxied a bit, and finally came to a halt, the captain announced: "Welcome to the Nam." They were in Vietnam. They landed at the U.S. Airbase at Bien Hoa. It was America's most active airbase at that particular time in the escalating Vietnam War. Located 20 miles outside of Saigon, the base held tremendous military and strategic importance. It was the jumping off point for American troop arrivals in the Nam.

The importance of the airbase did not escape America's and South Vietnam's nemesis, the North Vietnamese Army or NVA. There would be a lot of other names used for the enemy forces or NVA. Milton heard such derogatory names as the "Vietcong," "VC," "Charlie," and "Dink," to name a few. No one recalled him ever using any of those terms.

"What do you all think about the use of derogatory terms, calling one's enemy, your opponent, derogatory names?" Jamison asked the group.

Murphy was the first to respond. He said, "It was probably not right to call anyone a bad name just like today you know that you shouldn't use the N-word."

You could hear others, speaking in muffled voices in the background, saying that Murphy probably used the N-word himself and more than once and that others in the class were guilty too.

"Why do we use these derogatory terms for the enemy?" Jamison asked.

Several hands went up simultaneously, and he called on Jesus.

"We use these different names on them because we are fighting them and we don't want them to be thought of with respect," Jesus answered.

"Yes," Barbara added. "It is easier to fight against someone who you dislike or despise. So you call him names to belittle him and what he stands for."

Others nodded their heads in agreement.

The classroom's Barbara had expressed sentiments very similar to those expressed by another Barbara -- Barbara Spencer Penelton, Milton's cousin. When Milton wrote to her saying that his unit might see action, she cautioned him about his enthusiasm for the warrior tradition. Cousin Barbara was a maturing intellectual, a graduate of the University of

Illinois at Urbana-Champaign who became the first African American appointed to a faculty position at Bradley University in Peoria, Illinois. She was a bit older than Milton and far more informed about the escalating American involvement in Southeast Asia. She did not want to see her dear cousin caught up in what seemed to her to be the wrong side of what was happening.

Back to the ongoing exchange in the classroom, Murphy added to the conversation: "I know from my brother that over in Iraq and Afghanistan, many of our boys call the Arab and Muslim enemy 'Rag Heads.'"

"They also call them 'Sand N-word,'" Yousef blurted out.

"That's all true," Jamison confirmed to the group. He went on to say how during every war, the enemy was given derogatory names; how in

World War II the Germans were labeled as 'Krouts,' and told the class that was derived from sauerkraut, which was a favorite accompanying side dish that Germans ate. He also mentioned how the Japanese were referred to with stilted terms such as 'Japs' and 'Nips'" and that in the Korean War the Chinese combatants were given such awful names as 'Gooks' and 'Slopes.'

"All of you in this room have, I am certain, heard derogatory names for your own ethnic group," Jamison commented.

"We also called Native Americans, 'Redskins,' and other derogatory names," Jamison continued.

"But we still use the term Redskin today don't we?" Shanekwa asked and answered.

"Yes we do," Jamison replied. "What do you all think about that?"

"I don't care," Murphy said, "the Redskins are not that good of a football team anyhow!"

The group laughed. After the laughter died down, there was a serious discussion of terms used to describe and define Native Americans. Jamison pointed out to the students that many Native American groups find the terms used to describe and define them as offensive; that they are not 'Indians.'

He told them of the fight at his old alma mater, the University of Illinois, over its longtime mascot of Chief Illiniwek, with a student portraying a Native American, wearing native dress, war paint, and carrying a feather-covered spear. The "Chief" would do a war dance at half time of sporting events such as football and basketball, bringing the spectators to their feet with shouts and applause in tune with the Chief's war dance which he did center-stage on the field or court.

The movement to get rid of the Chief went on for over a decade at Illinois before a new administration and an overall more sensitive student body and Board of Trustees decided to drop the Chief.

"The University of Illinois," Jamison informed the group, "was still searching for a new and more appropriate and, if you like, 'politically correct' mascot."

The class also discussed for a bit the notion of political correctness, with Jamison and the students agreeing rather quickly that the term itself was misleading and in a sense offensive. It was not about being politically correct, the group decided. It was about being right and doing what was correct whether some thought it fashionable or not.

The sensitivity of the students struck Jamison, many of whom had little knowledge of the term and rarely heard it used. The group, however, thought it smacked of phoniness and could not see any value in the loaded and unnecessary jargon.

Many of the students came to a general agreement that the misuse of terms was wrong to do, and that it was wrong to use derogatory nicknames to belittle even an enemy. While most came to that conclusion, not all did, and Jamison could see it in that several of the students, like Murphy, simply stayed out of further debate rather than take on the large vocal segment of the group condemning the practice of using derogatory terms even during the Vietnam War. They understood why it was done and why it made opposition to a group or enemy more palatable. It was the old adage that it was easier to stamp out those that you did not respect nor see as fellow human-beings of equal worth.

Murphy finally spoke briefly and said that he also thought that you could fight people without putting them down. He said that he understood that whatever you called the NVA that they were some rugged opponents. "You have to give respect to a tough enemy, even if you don't like them; I think," Murphy concluded.

Then they turned their focus back to Milton in the Nam.

What struck Milton as they deplaned was the incredible heat and humidity of the place. You heard everyone talking about it. Despite the heat and humidity, commanders wanted the troopers to move out quickly to various points on the base and camps around it. Milton and the others heeded the orders not to bunch up together. He thought that likely had some significance. It most certainly did since the base there at Bien Hoa was not secure, to put it mildly.

All Milton knew was that he and his fellow Sky Soldiers were there to do their part in the Vietnam struggle and that the NVA were the anointed bad guys. What he learned soon was the primary object of the 173rd Airborne. The objective: to secure the perimeter of the airfield. Bien Hoa Airbase was frequently under mortar attack ever since the United States made it its primary jumping off point in Vietnam back in 1961. The problem of the mortar attacks had gotten worse over time. On 1 November 1964 the NVA peppered Bien Hoa with mortars late at night and into part of the early morning. Four U. S. soldiers and two Vietnamese allies were killed, and nineteen wounded. More than two dozen aircraft were damaged in that assault alone.

On 16 May 1965 there was a major explosion on the airbase that killed twenty-seven men and wounded more than one hundred. Twenty-six planes were destroyed. The NVA took credit for having hit their targets with mortars. An investigating committee of U. S. and Vietnamese military personnel concluded that the culprit was an accidental spark that set off a chain of explosions. Whatever the real cause, the U. S. military, in a confidential separate report, said that it could no longer rely on its Vietnamese allies to secure the perimeter. It was decided that U. S. forces needed to be brought in to provide perimeter security. Hence, the decision was made to deploy the 173rd Airborne Brigade to Vietnam to secure the Bien Hoa Airbase. That was the background to Milton's deployment. He and his comrades were told that they were there to make the area safe and to push back against the enemy.

The Bien Hoa Airbase was a largely flat region in a densely rural part of the countryside. To secure the perimeter all around the base meant that the 173rd would have to probe and push continuously against any enemy encroachment. The command concluded that it needed a three mile green zone. In other words, the security perimeter needed to be a complete circumference of at least three miles. To guarantee that level of security required constant patrols, probing of the enemy, continuous recon of the area, and search and destroy missions to push back or kill the NVA whenever they came in contact with them. It was, as the commanding officer of the 173rd explained it, "a seek, destroy, and secure mission," of which Milton was a part.

The assignment was no cake walk for the 173rd. The high command did not share information in terms of the number of casualties that U. S. forces and their allies suffered already in and around the airport and base. When Milton and his fellow troopers arrived, they could see, and were told by other soldiers, that they had lost men during their patrols into the bush. It was war and kill or be killed applied.

The burst of heat that Milton and the others were hit with when they first arrived was nothing like what it became when they experienced it day in and day out in the Nam. In full military gear, including helmet, backpack, extra ammunition and field rations, the only thing that did not seem to be an unbearable burden to Milton and the other guys were the M-14s that they carried, though the weapon was fairly heavy. (The M-16, introduced later in the war was much lighter, but the first version tended to jam – a disaster in a combat situation. The problem was eventually corrected.)

Milton and his fellow Sky Soldiers traveled with their weapons unloaded on the aircraft that got them to the Nam. After deplaning, the troopers were told to report first to the ammunition dispensing areas. Milton and the other troopers received five hundred rounds each. This was a clear indication that they were in a real shooting war. Training was over.

Lined up by company, Milton could see that there were units arriving continuously and pouring onto the base camp. The C-141s were all over the airfield, which indicated to him that he was one of more than two thousand-five hundred new arrivals. The war in Vietnam was ratcheting up. It was not full scale escalation as it would be soon enough. It was, however, a massive buildup taking place in that June of 1965, to which Milton contributed. Like all the others, he was assigned to a new unit, a new airborne command. He was still under the 173rd Airborne Brigade, 503rd Infantry, but now specifically assigned to Company B, 2nd Battalion, 3rd Platoon.

Milton's first few days in the Nam were full of briefings. The higher-ups wanted the men to have "the best understanding" of the type of war and enemy they were facing. Ironically, not much of Milton's training back at Fort Benning attempted to simulate dense brush encounters, especially the kind of jungles in which they were going to engage the enemy. Even if they had tried back at Fort Benning, no amount of training could have prepared him for the stultifying and debilitating heat and humidity. It was easily 100 degrees, and with the oppressive humidity it felt more like 110. It was for the Americans, a "bookoo baker" – – a towering inferno of discomfort that made it difficult to concentrate on objectives.

After hearing lectures, talks, and general and specific briefings from officers and seasoned enlisted men who had months and, in some cases, entire tours in the Nam under their belts, Milton was primed for his first patrol into the bush. What he did not know was that he was a replacement. The private first class whose place he took had been KIA (killed in action) four days earlier, along with two others of Company B. They were also beefing up the company in general with more "fresh meat" as the vets liked to call the new men.

He and the other replacements were helicoptered to the outer perimeters of the base, about two klicks (two kilometers) from the airbase and central operations. Milton's 3rd Platoon's guardian angel, or "mother hen," as the men affectionately referred to the platoon sergeant, was Vince Yrineo. Sergeant Yrineo was "old school" and 36 years of age at the time, the oldest man in the platoon and one of the most experienced sergeants in the entire company. Yrineo was a lifer, who pinned his foreseeable future on a career in the military. He was coming to the end of his first tour in Vietnam and was going to sign up for a second one because that was his calling. Sergeant Yrineo had a chest full of service ribbons, if he had bothered to display them which he did not. What was most important to him was getting the job done and keeping his men safe. He was the quintessential dedicated platoon sergeant. He did not wear his emotions on his sleeves. If he had, you would have known how deeply he felt about the young private of his platoon who was KIA days earlier, and whom Milton was now replacing. Given that the sergeant was Mexican-American, you knew that he knew his stuff and that no one had given him anything. Milton was fortunate for the experience of his sergeant. At the same time, it was clear that this was a platoon that regularly saw combat.

John "Hop" Foster was one of the members of the platoon that Milton got to know fairly well. They hit it off because they were nearly the same age. Hop was a year older, 19 years of age, a private, a black kid from Pittsburgh. He was a former boxer and played football in high school. In many respects he had been the athlete that Milton never was able to achieve for himself. Hop was a tough guy and it was clear he took no crap from anyone, no matter what their rank.

Lionel Hubbard, another member of the platoon, was an African American from Brownsville, Texas. He was a constant complainer about being in Vietnam and that he had nothing against the Vietnamese.

Nevertheless, it was well known that he was one of the toughest fighters in the platoon. Some referred to him as the old man because he was a full 20 years of age.

There was also George Gregorio Luis, who some thought was a black youngster from the South. Actually, Luis was Hawaiian. He was from Pahoa and another old-timer in that he was age 20. Milton immediately liked Luis because he was a pretty quiet guy like himself.

Milton did not develop any close bonds with any member of the platoon because he was so quiet. Several of the men labeled him "the preacher" because he was often found reading his Bible and he did not drink. But, unlike a preacher, he rarely preached to his comrades or cited Bible verse to them. Also, as a new replacement there was typically distance between him and the old-timers. Like most wars, there was a tendency not to make close bonds with newcomers. The close allegiance tended to be between those who came up or online around the same time.

Luckily for Milton, Sergeant Yrineo immediately liked him. The sergeant took into consideration the young man's diminutive size. He told Milton that size and the rest did not matter to him, that only results did and that no matter what your size, you could pull a trigger with the best of them and kill Charlie. Milton, like the rest of the American fighting forces in Vietnam, was for the most part gung-ho for the mission, despite complaining to one another on a rather frequent basis. According to those in power, America's fighting men were completely on board with the objective and united against the enemy.

Jamison reiterated details about Milton's deployment and first contact there in Vietnam.

The heat and humidity of the Nam were the least of the uncomfortableness of the environment. It was a war zone with an ever-increasing number of men on both sides fighting and dying.

Milton's first taste of combat came a little more than one week of his arrival in the Nam. It was his eighth day in base camp that Sergeant Yrineo called the platoon together to inform them that 3rd Platoon would be going into the bush before dawn the next morning on a reconnaissance mission.

A recon mission could be just as dangerous, or even more so, than a search and destroy mission. On recon, the idea was not to engage but to locate and report. The platoon would venture beyond the designated frontlines to see what information they could gather about the enemy. Where were they? How many? What were they doing? If the opportunity presented itself, the platoon on recon was to capture an enemy soldier or confiscate and retrieve any documents or other materials from the insurgents.

The irony of the term "insurgent" did not escape Jamison's students. Several of them immediately blurted out: "Who were the insurgents?" The Americans were the actual insurgents when you acknowledged whose country it was and what people were indigenous to the region. Jamison explained how the U. S. government and military leadership defined Vietnam into two regions: North and South, and how the Vietnamese from the north were defined as under the influence of Communist China and seen as bad for the South. He also informed them briefly about the Diem Regime and its pro-linkages to the U.S.

Returning to Milton Olive, Jamison pointed out how the young man was not knowledgeable of any of the intricate politics, intellectual debates, or reality of the nationalist movement of Ho Chi Minh and his followers. All Milton knew was the army line that America's friends in the South were being invaded by the Communists from the North. That was it for him and most of the GIs. In short, it was a straightforward and simple struggle of us versus them, of evil versus good, of communism versus democracy.

The morning of the recon mission came quickly. The eighteen men boarded the helicopter gunship before dawn and were air born to a designation that was three klicks from the northern edge of Phu Chong, a continuing trouble spot. Since their mission was recon, they would be at the tip of the spear of certain danger and contact with the enemy.

The helicopter pilot informed the lieutenant in charge of the platoon that he was about two minutes from touchdown. Yrineo relayed to the men a visual thumbs-up and then told them to "get frosty." Both the lieutenant and the sergeant reminded the men that when they jumped off to remember everything is hostile except your buddies. "We're on recon. We want to capture or seize documents. But don't let that get you killed. Watch out for land mines and other booby-traps. Remember your spacing. Remember your training." Then came the signal that Milton prepared for and waited for since the time he joined the army and after graduating as a Sky Soldier. Just before the helicopter set down, the lieutenant ordered the men to "Lock and load!" Sergeant Yrineo repeated the command: "Lock and load!"

The helicopter never completely touched down. It was standard practice in the Nam to hover a couple of feet from the ground in case it was necessary to abort and get out quickly. The men jumped out one or two at a time from the short distance and began immediately to fan out. Milton had his M-14 at the ready, with finger off the trigger and pointing straight. You were taught to always index and keep your finger off the trigger until it was absolutely necessary to fire. The military learned over the years that the extra second that it took to move the finger into the trigger housing allowed valuable time to be sure of your target and not merely to pull the trigger because something startled you. All government policing agencies learned from the military and adopted indexing or finger-pointing as standard proper procedure until required to use deadly force. The extra second saved many lives and resulted in far less friendly-fire shootings in Vietnam.

The platoon moved quickly to the north and deeper into enemy territory. Sergeant Yrineo was at the front. Once all the men cleared the open space, they came together to hear the commanding lieutenant's next directive. He spoke to the sergeant, telling him to put a man at point, and let's move it. The sergeant chose one of the men for point, then waited a bit and signaled quietly for the platoon to move out.

Point was one of those positions that no man volunteered for, and no one really wanted. The point person went substantially ahead of the unit with the thinking being that he would be the first to encounter the enemy. The point person was supposed to report back to the unit so that they would avoid disasters such as stumbling into an enemy stronghold or ambush.

The problem with the point position was that in the Nam, like in Korea or World War II, the opponents learned to allow the point to pass unharmed in order to ambush the main body of the unit. When the enemy was not waiting in ambush, the point person was the one most likely to draw fire. Hence, on point you had an excellent chance of being killed if you did not spot the enemy before he spotted you.

Third Platoon ventured about half a klick into the bush when the point came back to the unit, giving the password, and coming into the main body. He informed the lieutenant that he saw signs up ahead of enemy activity. He spotted what he believed to be a hooch or former campsite used by the NVA. Four men were ordered to return with the point to take a closer look and to report back.

There was no need to report back. In less than five minutes the scouting party was spotted by an enemy lookout and the NVA opened fire on them.

Hearing the gunfire, which included the unmistakable sound of AK-47s at work, the commander ordered the entire platoon to spread out and rapidly proceed forward to support the scouts, with three men left to trail at the rear to guard against a backdoor assault.

There had been much talk early on at the beginning of American intervention in Vietnam that the North Vietnamese soldiers, the so-called Vietcong, would run for cover when confronted by American fighting men. It proved to be totally untrue. In the later stages of the war, the North Vietnamese would adopt a strategy of hit-and-run rather than taking on American might and power directly. In the early stages of the war they took a frontal approach and defended their turf. They let the Americans know in no uncertain terms that this would be a fight to the death, or war they were prepared to either win or to all die fighting for their independence and freedom.

Third Platoon and Milton Olive were in a serious firefight. This was Milton's first real combat test. He did not freeze. He, like the others of the platoon, fired away shooting at the seen and unseen enemy. It is doubtful that Milton shot anyone in that encounter. Indeed it was doubtful that he ever shot or killed anyone while he served, although you can never be sure given the number of rounds fired. Also, the North Vietnamese, when possible, carried off not only their wounded but their dead as well. In that first combat encounter for Milton, four men of 3rd Platoon were wounded in battle.

After engaging in a firefight for what seemed an internally long period of time that was actually about five minutes, both units withdrew. Orders came for the platoon to proceed to the extraction point where they were going to be met by a couple of Hueys (helicopters) and be picked up and taken back to the base camp.

Milton had survived his first combat mission. When the unit arrived back at the base, the four wounded men were helped over to the M*A*S*H unit (mobile army surgical hospital) for medical attention. Prior to that, the medics did an excellent job in patching up the wounded and stabilizing their injuries. All the men talked about was their firefight with the insurgents. While the platoon commander and the sergeant reported for debriefing, the men were ordered to stand down and to get some rest. Most were too hyped up to get any rest. There would be a great deal of drinking and equally great deal of smoking of marijuana.

Jamison informed the students that the use of marijuana was widespread among American troops in Vietnam. He also informed them that there were some critics who argued later that the use of drugs made the men less effective in their fighting. At the same time, Jamison told the class, there were those who argued that the use of liquor and marijuana helped make the war bearable as it was such a nasty, hot, humid, and intense struggle. He could have entertained a lot of questions about that since hands went up. Jamison decided not to and then resumed the story with the students eagerly listening to Milton's next combat mission.

At the base camp they did a one-day on and one-day off whether it was recon or search and destroy. It meant for Milton and his platoon that they would be standing down all day tomorrow and could use that time to relax as much as possible. While others did their drinking and smoking, Milton spent much of that time reading his Bible. Thus reinforcing the nickname of "the preacher."

In Milton's very next mission he and his platoon engaged in another firefight. This time their objective was search and destroy, which meant exactly what it said. The job was to go out, engage the enemy, and kill or capture any NVA with which they came into contact. They were also part of a parameter sweep, or house cleaning as some liked to call it, and would not be helicoptered anyplace. They started from the base camp as other units were doing and fanned out to secure the area. The airbase was still the target of occasional mortar rounds, which meant that the enemy was finding ways to get in close. Thus the 173rd was sweeping the area from the airbase to their campsite and then three klicks beyond that to extend the green safety zone perimeter.

Milton's platoon was less than one klick from the base camp before they found themselves under heavy enemy fire. They called in artillery support to shell the area a few hundred yards in front of them. The firefighting continued and in the exchange Milton's unit killed at least three NVA. They know this for a fact because they found the bodies on this occasion. But in this long running gun-battle which went on for a good thirty minutes, two members of Milton's platoon were injured, he being one of them.

The unit broke off engagement when there was no more fire coming from the enemy locale. One of the platoon's medics attended to Milton and the other soldier wounded in the action. Milton's was only a flesh wound to his left arm yet it bled profusely. He was as frightened as could be when he saw his own blood. Milton's wound in that firefight earned him the Purple Heart Medal.

You might think that he would have immediately written home about his experience and the commendation it earned him. He did not. Milton did not want to alarm his family and certainly not his grandparents in Lexington. Instead, he wrote to his grandmother and asked her to please send him some cookies. In that letter he told her everything was going fine. He did mention that they engaged the enemy on a number of occasions but that American firepower was superior and the enemy was forced to withdraw. He conveyed much the same to his father in Chicago, although he made no request to him for cookies.

After getting his wound tended to back at the base and later receiving his Purple Heart, Milton and his entire unit were given a double dose of time off to relax, recuperate, and re-energize. Their unit had taken on the toughest firefight during the week and the commanding officer of the base camp gave the group a reward of a few extra days of downtime.

Those days went past quickly. Milton's platoon was soon back online and performing their tasks with a routine schedule, going deep into the bush and engaging the enemy wherever they encountered him. What was different was they had a new commanding officer for the platoon. His name was Lieutenant Jimmy Stanford from Texas.

Stanford, like Yrineo, was a lifer who was making a career of the military. He was 29 years of age, which was a good sign. That he was a full lieutenant rather than a second lieutenant was another good sign. Both age and rank indicated that he likely knew what he was doing. Second lieutenants as a rule, did not last long in the Nam. Many who were fresh out of West Point or some other military academy were unseasoned and generally unprepared for action in Vietnam. There was an ongoing joke of sorts that any second lieutenant who lasted more than a month or two in the Nam needed to be promoted. Too often a wet behind the ears 2nd "Louie" would get himself killed and many of his men.

Second lieutenants, and any officer with insignia displayed, were favorite targets of NVA snipers. They always went first for those wearing rank, and since second lieutenants were typically high visible officers with platoons, they had a short life expectancy. Those who survived the initial encounters with the enemy learned to take off their rank insignia and have their men refrain from saluting them.

"It was what you did," Jamison explained to the students, "if you wanted to increase your chances of survival."

That First Lieutenant Stanford was a survivor, and had risen through the ranks, told his men that their chances of staying alive were better than most. The combination of a seasoned lieutenant and a crafty well experienced sergeant bode well for 3rd Platoon. Unfortunately, the new Lieutenant and his platoon never got the chance to bond together before being sent out in what proved to be the unit's most harrowing firefight.

Milton's cookies from his grandmother did not arrive in time.

Chapter VI:
Step Forward the Hero

The offensive on 22 October 1965 was a major one on the part of Company B, 503rd Infantry, 173rd Airborne Brigade. Helicopters picked up the entire 2nd Battalion just before the crack of dawn. Milton and 3rd Platoon, along with the others, were deposited at the outer edge of Phu Cuong in the green zone perimeter. The various units immediately fanned out. No sooner than they took a few paces the NVA let loose with a devastating barrage of fire. Some men were injured in that exchange but the platoon pushed on. Only a few more paces beyond the burned out clearing, a sniper shot ringed out and hit its mark. George Gregorio Luis was struck in the head and killed instantly. There was no time to mourn his loss, however. The entire unit was in a life-and-death struggle.

The platoon kept pushing its way forward, beyond the clearing into the thick jungle where they had to machete their way through the bush. They continued to press forward. The exchange of gunfire never stopped. This was a search and destroy mission and Stanford and his men were determined to do exactly that. They kept up the relentless firing, and the enemy returned in kind.

At one point in the exchange, the NVA hurriedly retreated. The platoon chased them further into the bush. Telling the platoon to spread out, Stanford and four other men, Yrineo, Foster, Hubbard, and Milton took off in hot pursuit of the retreating NVA. They must have pursued them for about 100 yards before all hell broke loose. They had run into a classic V ambush with the five of them at the lower point of the formation and the enemy directly in front of them and on the upper edge of their left and right flanks -- a perfect crossfire.

The NVA were firing at them from seemingly every direction, on the ground and from trees. The rest of the platoon was coming up behind Stanford and his men on the left and right but all were now under tremendous fire. Lieutenant Stanford, Sergeant Yrineo, and Privates Hop Foster, Lionel Hubbard, and Milton were so thoroughly pinned down that the best they could do was to lift their weapons slightly above their heads and fire blindly in the general direction of the enemy. To have lifted your head up even a little bit would have cost you your life. If you were fortunate enough to be by a tree stump you kept your head pinned down behind it as low as you could possibly get. If you were in the flat area on the ground you hugged the earth for all it was worth while still trying to hold your hand up a bit and fire your weapon. They were in deep trouble and doing all that they could to keep the enemy off of them.

Grenades were being tossed by each force against the other. Stanford and his men were in a relatively tight perimeter and would raise their hands just quick enough to throw grenades in the direction of the enemy. The enemy was already responding in kind. One of the grenades from the NVA landed in the midst of the five men. Milton yelled "Look out Lieutenant, grenade!" And with no hesitation, Milton grabbed the device and fell on it, smothering it with his body. The grenade immediately exploded and tossed him a foot or more into the air, flipping him over on his back.

The other men were dazed by the blast and suffered shrapnel wounds, some more severe than others. Milton, however, took the full measure of the explosion. He was killed instantly.

The rest of the platoon caught up with the five and gave a continuous barrage of suppressing fire that allowed for Stanford and the other survivors to be extracted. One man lost several toes from the grenade blast and the other four were hit and seriously wounded by shrapnel that imbedded into their bodies. Yrineo and Hubbard had to be carried out of the bush. But they all lived thanks to Milton's heroism and sacrifice.

The injured men were carried back to the helicopter drop site. They also retrieved Milton's body. One member of the team who assisted in extracting the bodies was Robert Toporek, who later wrote of how the entire experience of Milton's bravery helped to change his life. Milton's remains, along with those of George Luis, were tagged and bagged, as they referred to it in the Nam, and taken back on the helicopter to the base camp. They were not the only Americans killed during the operation. The company loss other men that day.

It was during Lieutenant Stanford's debriefing that he recounted to the company commanding officer the exceptional valor displayed by Milton. Stanford's account and the confirmation from Sergeant Yrineo and Private Hubbard from their hospital beds persuaded the company commander to put forth Milton's name, and act of heroism, for exceptional commendation.

Yrineo would lose a total of eight of his men during his tour in Vietnam. No act of sacrifice or heroism would stand out more to him than that of

Milton.   The sergeant would forever keep Milton's battered dog tag as a precious reminder and tribute to the "little black kid from Chicago who saved our lives."

It remained that the family had to be notified back in Chicago that their son would not be coming home.   Grandma Olive in Mississippi sensed that something was terribly wrong when the cookies she mailed to Milton earlier in October were returned to her with no explanation. It was Antoinette Olive, Milton's stepmother who, while preparing dinner one evening later in the month, heard the doorbell ring and paused from her cooking to go and answer it.

There was a man dressed neatly in a dark suit and carrying a small attaché case.   When she answered the door, he identified himself as a member of the U. S. Military and said that he had a letter for her.   The man then asked was there someone else at the house who could be with her for the reading of the letter. She knew it must be bad news. Her husband, Milton Olive senior, would not be home for several hours.

She took her seat and asked the man to read her the letter. He did not read it. Instead, he gave it to her since it was sealed and addressed to the family of Milton Lee Olive, III. Milton's stepmother opened the letter gingerly. The opening sentence foretold what was coming: "I regret to inform you." The letter was what she expected. It informed her that her son had given his life for his country and that the family should be proud of his heroic service to the United States of America.

Thankfully she read the letter while sitting. The bad news took her breath away and she felt faint. She remembered very little after that. A short while later, Milton's father came home and his wife broke the unbearably bad news to him. They hugged and wept together. Their son Milton was gone.

Six days later, Milton's body was returned home. Milton's father, in consultation with the grandparents in Mississippi, decided to bury his son in Lexington. Milton Lee Olive, III, was put to rest in the black cemetery near the Pentecostal church and school that he once attended. At the funeral were Milton's father and stepmother, grandparents, Lee family relatives of his biological mother, and friends and neighbors of Lexington. It was an open-coffin service. The grenade explosion miraculously did not hit Milton's face.

Over the coming weeks and months, Milton's father received more details about his son's sacrifice in Vietnam and incredible heroism. They were told of his Purple Heart Medal and other citations for valor. They were also informed that the company commanding officer and his superiors were recommending to the President of the United States that Milton be awarded the Medal of Honor for his great courage.

Six months later, Milton's family was joined by Lieutenant Jimmy Stanford, Private John Foster, and Chicago Mayor Richard J Daley, in Washington as special guests at the White House. On 21 April 1966, President Lyndon Baines Johnson presented Milton's father with the nation's highest military commendation, the Medal of Honor, awarded posthumously to his son, Milton Lee Olive, III. President Johnson spoke:

"Mr. and Mrs. Olive, members of the Olive family, distinguished Mayor Daley, Secretary

Resor, General Wheeler, Members of the Senate, Members of the House, ladies and gentlemen:

There are occasions on which we take great pride, but little pleasure. This is one such occasion. Words can never enlarge upon acts of heroism and duty, but this Nation will never forget Milton Lee Olive III.

President Harry Truman once said that he would far rather have won the Medal of Honor than to have been the President of the United States. I know what he meant. Those who have earned this decoration are very few in number. But true courage is very rare. This honor we reserve for the most courageous of all of our sons.

The Medal of Honor is awarded for acts of heroism above and beyond the call of duty. It is bestowed for courage demonstrated not in blindly overlooking danger, but in meeting it with eyes clearly open.

That is what Private Olive did. When the enemy's grenade landed on that jungle trail, it was not merely duty which drove this young man to throw himself upon it, sacrificing his own life that his comrades might continue to live. He was compelled by something that is more than duty, by something greater than a blind reaction to forces that are beyond his control.

He was compelled, instead, by an instinct of loyalty which the brave always carry into conflict. In that incredibly brief moment of decision in which he decided to die, he put others first and himself last. I have always believed that to be the hardest, but the highest, decision that any man is ever called upon to make.

In dying, Private Milton Olive taught those of us who remain how we ought to live.

I have never understood how men can ever glorify war. "The rockets' red glare, the bombs bursting in air," has always been for me better poetry than philosophy. When war is foisted upon us as a cruel recourse by men who choose force to advance policy, and must, therefore, be resisted, only the irrational or the callous, and only those untouched by the suffering that accompanies war, can revel.

Let us never exult over war. Let us not for one moment disguise in the grandest justifications of policy the inescapable fact that war feeds on the lives of young men, good young men like Milton Olive. I can never forget it. I am reminded of it every moment of every day. In a moment such as this, I am reminded all over again how brave the young are, and how great is our debt to them, and how endless is the sacrifice that we call upon them to make for us.

I realize, too, how highly we prize freedom-when we send our young to die for it.

There are times when Vietnam must seem to many a thousand contradictions, and the pursuit of freedom there an almost unrealizable dream.

But there are also times--and for me this is one of them--when the mist of confusion lifts and the basic principles emerge:

--that South Vietnam, however young and frail, has the right to develop as a nation, free from the interference of any other power, no matter how mighty   or   strong;

--that the normal processes of political action, if given time and patience and freedom to work, will some day, some way create in South Vietnam a society that is responsive to the people and consistent with their traditions;

--that aggression by invading armies or ruthless insurgency must be denied the precedent of success in Vietnam, if the many other little nations in the world, and if, as a matter of fact, all Southeast Asia is to ever know genuine order and unexploited change;

--that the United States of America is in South Vietnam to resist that aggression and to permit that peaceful change to work its way, because we desire only to be a good and honorable ally, a dependable, trustworthy friend, and always a sincere and genuine servant of peace.

Men like Milton Olive die for honor. Nations that are without honor die, too, but without purpose and without cause. It must never be said that when the freedom and the independence of a new and a struggling people were at stake this mighty, powerful Nation of which we are so proud to be citizens would ever turn aside because we had the harassments that always go with conflict, and because some thought the outcome was uncertain, or the course too steep, or the cost too high.

In all of this there is irony, as there is when any young man dies. Who can say what words Private Olive might have chosen to explain what he did? Jimmy Stanford and John Foster, two of the men whose lives he saved that day on that lonely trail in that hostile jungle 10,000 miles from here are standing on the White House steps today because this man chose to die. I doubt that even they know what was on his mind as he jumped and fell across that grenade.

But I think I do know this: On the sacrifices of men who died for their country and their comrades, our freedom has been built. Whatever it is that we call civilization rests upon the merciless and seemingly irrational fact of history that some have died for others to live, and every one of us who enjoys freedom at this moment should be a witness to that fact.

So Milton Olive died in the service of a country that he loved, and he died that the men who fought at his side might continue to live. For that sacrifice his Nation honors him today with its highest possible award.

He is the eighth Negro American to receive this Nation's highest award. Fortunately, it will be more difficult for future presidents to say how many Negroes have received the Medal of Honor. For unlike the other seven, Private Olive's military records have never carried the color of his skin or his racial origin, only the testimony that he was a good and loyal citizen of the United States of America.

So I can think of no more fitting tribute to him than to read from a letter that was written to me by this patriot's father, dated March 10.

'It is our dream and prayer that some day the Asiatics, the Europeans, the Israelites, the Africans, the Australians, the Latins, and the Americans can all live in One-World. It is our hope that in our own country the Klansmen, the Negroes, the Hebrews, and the Catholics will sit down together in the common purpose of good will and dedication; that the moral and creative intelligence of our united people will pick up the chalice of wisdom and place it upon the mountain top of human integrity; that all mankind, from all the earth, shall resolve, 'to study war no more.' That, Mr. President, is how I feel and that is my eternal hope for our Great American Society.'

Ladies and gentlemen, I have no words to add to that."

[Secretary of the Army Stanley R. Resor read the citation, the text of which follows.]

CITATION

"THE PRESIDENT of the United States of America, authorized by Act of Congress, March 3, 1863, has awarded in the name of The Congress the Medal of Honor, posthumously, to

PRIVATE FIRST CLASS MILTON L. OLIVE, III UNITED STATES ARMY

for conspicuous gallantry and intrepidity in action at the risk of his life above and beyond the call of duty:

Private First Class Milton L. Olive, III, distinguished himself by conspicuous gallantry and intrepidity at the risk of his own life above and beyond the call of duty while participating in a search and destroy operation in the vicinity of Phu Cuong, Republic of Vietnam, on 22 October 1965. Private Olive was a member of the 3d Platoon of Company B, 2d Battalion (Airborne), 503d Infantry, as it moved through the jungle to find the Viet Cong operating in the area. Although the Platoon was subjected to a heavy volume of enemy gun fire and pinned down temporarily, it retaliated by assaulting the Viet Cong positions, causing the enemy to flee. As the Platoon pursued the insurgents, Private Olive and four other soldiers were moving through the jungle together when a grenade was thrown into their midst. Private Olive saw the grenade, and then saved the lives of his fellow soldiers at the sacrifice of his own by grabbing the grenade in his hand and failing on it to absorb the blast with his body. Through his bravery, unhesitating actions, and complete disregard for his own safety, he prevented additional loss of life or injury to the members of his platoon. Private Olive's conspicuous gallantry, extraordinary heroism, and intrepidity at the risk of his own life above and beyond the call of duty are in the highest traditions of the United States Army and reflect great credit upon himself and the Armed Forces of his country."

After a long silence pause, Jamison said to the
sixteen students sequestered there in his
classroom in the Milton L Olive Middle School,
"President Johnson's words should be taken to
heart. Even more so, we need to heed the words
of Milton's father when he said, let us 'study war
no more.' He was telling us that war, that
fighting, is the last resort, and should be avoided
at all costs. I want you students to keep that in
mind. Do you really want to kill or hurt one
another? I want you to think about the
opportunity that Milton L Olive did not have and
that you do have. I want you to think about this
school, named in his honor and memory, and
what your responsibility should be to make his
sacrifice meaningful. You have the chance, the
opportunity, indeed the responsibility to do

something good with your lives. Don't waste the opportunity. Get an education. Advance from here to high school to college and beyond. I want to see each and every one of you as productive citizens of the United States of America.

"Milton gave his life for his country and what he believed in. The war in Vietnam went on for many more years until the signing of the Paris Peace Accords in 1973 and withdrawal of American troops. Final hostilities ended in 1975. Many Americans agreed with the war but many Americans disagreed with it and protested against it. If you agree with your nation's policies great. If you do not agree with them that's great too. Work to change them. But you can only be a player if you are educated and serious about making a difference and contributing to society.

"I think I've said enough. Hopefully you've got the message of our exchange this afternoon.

And thank you for sharing some of your thoughts and ideas with me."

Yousef's hand went up and Jamison hesitatingly acknowledged him.

"Mister Jamison," Yousef said, "If we had more teachers like you I think I would actually like history."

The students broke out into light laughter after Yousef's remarks.

Then Murphy and several others began saying thank you as well to Mr. Jamison.

"I'm flattered Yousef and to all of you. Thank you so much," Jamison responded. "And please continue to probe and ask those critical questions. All of you, continue to question everything around you and find your own truth and positive direction. Please!"

Jamison told the group that he had nothing more to add. He thanked them again for their attention and said that class was dismissed and they were free to leave.

The students rose quietly and respectfully from their chairs and started moving toward the door to go home when Shanekwa blurted out that she had one final question. Jamison told her to please go ahead with it. Everyone paused.

"Mister J, What makes a hero?" She asked with absolute inquisitiveness and earnest.

Jamison thanked her for the question, gave it some thought, and then answered: "I think it is a combination of factors that go into the making of a hero: upbringing, beliefs, personality, and character. It's hard to say. In the end, the actions speak louder than words. What we know for certain is that in the case of Milton Olive, and other heroes, that there are those individuals who, unlike many people who do nothing or run away from or step back from great danger or extreme crisis, the hero steps forward."

Suggested Further Reading:

Samuel W. Black, *Soul Soldiers: African Americans and the Vietnam Era* (Philadelphia, PA: Historical Society of Western Pennsylvania, 2006)

Lawrence A. Eldridge, *Chronicles of a Two-Front War: Civil Rights and Vietnam in the African American Press* (Columbia, MO: University of Missouri Press, 2012)

Ed Emanuel, *Soul Patrol* (New York, NY: Presidio Press, 2003)

Charles E. Neu, *America's Lost War: Vietnam: 1945-1975* (Wheeling, IL: Harlan Davidson, Inc., 2005)

John Darrell Sherwood, *Black Sailor, White Navy: Racial Unrest in the Fleet during the Vietnam War Era* (New York, NY: New York University Press, 2007)

Wallace Terry, *Bloods: Black Veterans of the Vietnam War: An Oral History* (New York, NY: Ballantine Books, 1985)

James E. Westheide, *Fighting on Two Fronts: African Americans and the Vietnam War* (New York, NY: New York University Press, 1997)